Samir Karmieh, Łukasz Gł

PANZER II & LUCHS
The World War II German Basic Light Tank

Instead of an introduction

In the initial stage of the II World War the Panzerkampfwagen II light tanks of various variants and types made the core of the Third Reich's armoured divisions. Vehicles of this group took part in almost every campaign in which the German Wehrmacht fought, what is very unsual for armoured fighting vehicles of the last, global conflict. The enemies of the Adolf Hitler's state faced those machines in the wilderness of Poland and the Soviet Union, in the mountains of Norway and the Balkans, as well as on the fields of France or deserts in North Africa. Despite this fact, these tracked fighting vehicles, many of which lighter than 11 tons, are usually put on the back burner in comparison to less numerous but commonly regarded as more effective and spectacular medium tanks Pz.Kpfw. V Panter or heavy tanks Pz.Kpfw. VI Tiger. It is worth remembering and mentioning that if the Germans had not gained so much experience with popular Panzer II, the development of Panzerwaffe would have not been so rapid and dynamic. Even this fact makes this group of tanks worthy of devoting a little more attention than usual.

This publication is focused on the history of the construction and combat use of all the 17 versions of Pz.Kpfw. II, as well as those, that came into being only on the drawing tables or as prototypes that have not entered series production. The author hopes that the knowledge concentrated and gathered in the following pages would allow the reader to synthetically and accesibly familiriaze with the history of changes of the said vehicle group, as well as its tactical usage on the battlefield. Moreover, a part of the study is dedicated to the Ausf. L "Luchs" [German: "lynx"] vehicle, which today might be considered as the marginal and secondary development trend of the Pz.Kpfw. II. It drawed the author's attention mainly because of its typical structure, as well as because its fate was, in a way, the crown of the German light tanks in 1944.

Koszalin, September 2016.

Panzer II & Luchs. The World War II German Basic Light Tank • Samir Karmieh, Łukasz Gładysiak • First edition • LUBLIN 2016

© All English Language Rights Reserved. With the exception of quoting brief passages for the purposes of review, no part of this publication may be reproduced without prior written permission from the Publisher. Nazwa serii zastrzeżona w UP RP • **ISBN 978-83-65437-43-3**

Editors: **Łukasz Gładysiak** • Photo: **Archive of Kagero, Bundesarchiv**
Photo caption: **Łukasz Gładysiak** • Color profiles: **Arkadiusz Wróbel** • Cover image: **Arkadiusz Wróbel / Samir Karmieh**
• Design: **KAGERO STUDIO, Marcin Wachowicz**

KAGERO Publishing
Akacjowa 100, Turka, os. Borek, 20-258 Lublin 62, Poland, phone/fax: (+48) 81 501 21 05
www.kagero.pl • e-mail: kagero@kagero.pl, marketing@kagero.pl
w w w . k a g e r o . p l

Pz.Kpfw. II Ausf. A-C of the unknown unit of Panzergruppe Guderian passing a destroyed BA-6 Soviet armored car during the Operation Barbarossa; eastern front, summer 1941. Note the spare track links used as an additional armor of the hull [Kagero Archive].

CHAPTER I

History of the light tanks development

In the first part of the 30s in the 20th century, the new chapter of the German history has opened – of the Germany that was facing more than only an economical crysis. On 30th January 1933, the office of chancellor of the, at that time still, republic, was taken by the leader of the National Socialist German Worker's Party (NSDAP) – Adolf Hitler. In a short time the supporters of the superpower politics, braking with the resolutions imposed on the Berlin on the strength of the Treaty of Versailles, signed in 1919, seized both power and control of the country. The birth of the Third Reich was proclaimed, with Hitler acting as the Leader (Führer), at the head of the state. Any restriction, supervised by the international community, was rejected and turned down, what clearly and unambiguosly led Germany on the path towards a new war.

In those fervent and ardent times, even before announcing the restoration of the compulsory military service and setting up Wehrmacht in place of the Republican Armed Forces, a new armoured divisions development programme was launched in Berlin. Soon, the assembly lines began producing light tanks Pz.Kpfw. I Ausf. A and the prolonged, developmental version – Ausf. B, which in larger and larger amounts joined the ranks of new Panzerwaffe sub-units, formed over and over again. Shortly afterwards it turned out, among others during field manoeuvres in various parts of the Third Reich, that in case of escalation of armed conflict with two basic enemies: Poland on the east and France on the west, these vehicles might turn out to be inefficient in combat. One of the main weaknesses and foibles of the Pz.Kpfw. I was the armament consisting of only two 7,92 mm machine guns Maschinengewehr 13, which performed well against enemy infantry, but made quite a poor opponent for the enemy tanks.

Front line tanks

In July 1934 the VI Department of the Army Weapons Agency (Heereswaffenamt) issued an order to create plans of a vehicle weighting approximately 10 000 kg – in the shortest period possible. This vehicle was meant to support the front line armoured troops. This project, just like all the previous military projects, was concealed and code-named "Farming tractor 100" (Landwirtschaftlicher Schlepper 100 or LaS 100), marking it also as Versuchs Kraftfahrzeug 622 [German: Experimental vehicle 622]. The addressees of this directive were 4 companies: Friedrich Krupp AG with seat in Essen, Henschel und Söhn in Kassel, Nuremberg Maschinenfabrik Augsburg-Nürnberg (MAN) and Daimler Benz AG at Berlin-Marienfeld. In October 1935 the first of the abovementioned factories presented a prototype marked as LKA II. It was the developmental version of Pz.Kpfw. I Ausf. A with larger, manually turned turret, armed 7,92 mm MG 13 machine gun and with quick-firing cannon Kampfwagenkanone (KwK) 30 L/55, cal. 20 mm, which was a commonly used anti-aircraft cannon Flugabwehrkanone 30, cal. 20 mm, converted for use in armoured fighting vehicles. Soon the other companies – MAN and Henschel – presented their proposals, and this solution, consisting of three bogies, two road wheels [sometimes called also "suspension wheels"] each, was approved for production. The turret was taken from the Krupp company's project.

The new, German light tank was labeleed as 2 cm Maschinengewehr Panzerwagen and after a new armywide terminology was established – its name changed to Panzerkampfwagen II Ausf.a Sonderkraftfahrzeug (Sd.Kfz.) 121. The powerplant of this vehicle, which total mass amounted to 7600 kg, was a six-cyllinder, 130 HP Maybach HL57TR petrol engine, of almost 5700 ccm displacement, capable to accelerate the vehicle to maximum road speed of 40 km/h (29 mph). The fuel – classic, German military 74-octane petrol was stored in two tanks – first one containig 102 liters and the second one – 68 liters. It granted the range 210 km on road or 160 km in cross country – in one tank. The three-person crew was protected by a 13 mm armour, but the yoke of the main armament was protected by a casted plate 15 mm thick. The decision to launch the series production was made along with rearmament of the Germany, announced in autumn of 1935. The first machines, labelled as Ausf.a1 left the MAN production plant in May, next year. In the end, there were three series, 25 vehicles each: Ausf. a1, Ausf.a2 and Ausf.a3 – and their hull number plates covered numbers from 20001 to 20075.

Every batch of the Pz.Kpfw. II Ausf.a had unique characteristics, that simultaniously made a mark of the search for optimal technical solutions for the new Panzerwaffe vehicle. The distinctive feature of the first 10 Ausf.a1 machines was the cast idler wheel with a rubber tire, which was in the end replaced with welded one, without the tire. In the Ausf. a2 variant, the fire barrier was added, which insulated the powerplant section from the fighting compartment and a wider inspection lid, granting access to the fuel system. Crews performing maintenance of these tanks noticed the need to improve ventilation and that problem was addresses quickly as well. Moreover, the radiator system of the power generator, delivered traditionally by the Bosch company, was also improved. The last series – Ausf. a3 had bigger radiator and reinforced shock absorbers.

Pz.Kpfw. II Ausf. C photographed during the Polish campaign in September 1939. The national emblem, white Balkenkreuz on the turret side painted over with a darker color or a thick layer of mud – probably to avoid being spotted by the enemy artillery. Note lack of one of the road wheels [Kagero Archive].

Between February and March 1937 next 25 tanks left the Nuremberg assembly lines, this time marked as Pz.Kpfw. II Ausf.b (sometimes one can find also version Ausf.a4 but because of many reasons such numbering seems incorrect). Vehicles, which hull number plates covered numbers 21001 – 21025 were equipped with stronger, 140 HP Maybach HL62TR engine, 6324 ccm displacement – because its larger fuel consumption the range fell by respectively by 20 and 35 km. Moreover, the power transmission system and gearbox were also improved, the drive wheel of new type was installed, as well as smaller return rollers. Installing wider tracks created demand for suitable road wheels and return rollers, although the hull system, created by Henschl factory, remained unchanged. All the modifications resulted in gaining weight

Pz.Kpfw. II Ausf. A-C of the Panzer-Regiment 25 belonging to the general Erwin Rommel's 7th Armored Division during the French campaign in May 1940. Note the large tactical number painted on the turret side and the Balkenkreuz national emblem as well as the yellow divisional insignia painted on the rear plate [Kagero Archive].

Pz.Kpfw. II Ausf. C belonging to the 25th Armored Regiment of the 7th Panzer Division during maneuvers in Germany, winter 1939 or 1940. The rounded front hull part was typical of this version. It was finally changed in the Ausf. D and later models [Kagero Archive].

– the vehicle became 500 kg heavier. Moreover, the rear mudguards were desgined as a separate, liftable component, so that it was easier to remove, for example, mud; once more the fresh air inlet system was improved – both to the fighting compartment and the engine bay.

The Pz.Kpfw. II Ausf.b tanks were the first of the light, tracked Wehrmacht fighting vehicles, that were subsequently modernized in many ways. First modernization, invented by engineers of Magirus factory located in Ulm, was introduced already at the beginning of 1940 – they mounted a two-piece folding bridge on a turretless hull [such construction later became known as the vehicle-launched bridge]. At least 4 such vehicles, marked as Brückenleger auf Panzerkampfwagen II were used in May and June, the same year, on the eastern front, in ranks of the 7th Panzer Division. The next variant consisted of demolition vehicle (called also: self-propelled mine or beetle tank) Ladungsleger II, of which at least one was delievered to the 58th engineering battalion of the 7th Panzer Division. Other vehicles were allegedly used as mineploughs and maintenance vehicles, transporting spare parts and tools. Just like in the case of Pz.Kpfw. II Ausf. A, Ausf. B and Ausf. C, in the summer 1941 the engineers tried to rearm Ausf. b version from standard 20 mm KwK 30 gun with trophy French cannon Sa 38, cal. 37 mm. This version never came to life and remained a theoretical project only.

The intensive trials on testing grounds, carried out in Germany right before the outbreak of the II World War, made clear that the Henschl hull and suspension was quite prone to breakdowns. That being so, in March 1937 the MAN factory presented first of the batch consisting of 25 vehicles of the next version – Pz.Kpfw II Ausf.c. Its distinctive feature was the suspension system consisting of 5 singular independently sprung larger steel wheels with rubber tires and 4 return rollers on each side of the tank. The return rollers were widened, what forced the creation of new version of the idler and tank's fenders. This model was probably treated as temporary solution – as a proof of this theory researchers often point out the fact, that both the fuselage and the turret were made of molybdenum steel, which was of worser quality, compared to the standards.

The same hull was introduced to the next group of Pz.Kpfw II: Ausf.A (series production of July – December 1937 period), Ausf.B (December 1937 – June 1938) and Ausf.C (June 1938 – April 1940), which was the largest batch of this tank (totalling 1113 vehicles, hull number plates 21101 – 27000). The assembly of these tanks took place not only in Maschinenfab-

Pz.Kpfw. II Ausf. A-C crossing the Austrian border during the Anschluss (annexation) of Austria, spring 1938. The vehicle represented the standard, mono-tone, Panzergrau camouflage pattern and small, white tactical number put down in a black field - typical feature of the Panzerwaffe tanks in the second half of the 30s. Note the lack of Balkenkreuz national emblem that was usually painted on the superstructure or turret side [Kagero Archive].

Panzer II & Luchs. The World War II German Basic Light Tank

Field graves of two Pz.Kpfw. II Ausf. A-C crews. Their tanks were destroyed probably during the French campaign in May or June 1940 [Kagero Archive].

rik Augsburg-Nürnberg production plant, but also in Henschl factory, Wegmann Co. in Kassel, Altmärkische Kettenfabrik GmbH (Alkett) in Berlin-Spandau, Mühlenbau und Industrie AG Amme-Werk in Braunschweig (MIAG) and in Fahrzeug- und Motorenwerke GmbH (FAMO) in Wrocław [Breslau]. All of them of course cooperated with the main supplier of the hulls – the Daimler-Benz AG factories in Berlin.

The front armour was thickened to 14,5 mm but it turned out during fighting against Polish Army in September and October 1939 that it inadequately protected the 3 crew members of the tank. That being so, beggining with May 1940, the Germans began riveting additional 20 mm thick steel sheets to the glacis plate and the turret. The author of numerous publications on German armoured vehicles of the 20th century, Peter Chamberlain, established that this solution was applied to around 70% of all Ausf. A-Ausf. C vehicles. Apart from the modification of the suspension system, the engine was also modified, by installing the Maybach HL62TRM engine (140 HP) as well as the synchronized gearbox Zahnradfabrik Aphon SSG46. An interesting thing here is that in November 1938 the Nuremberg factory began trials of the new, compression-ignition powerplant HWA 1038G, which was supposed to reach power of 200 HP but it was cancelled without any positive results towards the end of the second year of the war. All said modifications

Formerly belonging to Panzer-Abteilung 90 of 90th Light Division Pz.Kpfw. II Ausf. F captured by the American 1st Ranger Battalion near El Guattar. The insignia presented in the photograph had been added by the capturers, as well as the "SNAFU" nickname. Note the additional pennants, one of which says: "North African Branch Armored Force School". Tunisia, spring 1943 [Kagero Archive].

Pz.Kpfw. II Ausf. C during a parade in an unknown German town, probably just after the victory over France, late spring 1940. Note the typical turret with flat, two-part commander's hatch, 2,0 cm KwK 30 main gun and coaxial 7,92 mm machine gun MG 13 [Kagero Archive].

caused that the weight of the Pz.Kpfw. II in the described group increased to 8,9 t.

When describing the Ausf. A, Ausf. B and Ausf. C versions, it is worth to mention one of the most interesting tank modifications that came into being in the Third Reich, that is the amphibious aka swimming tank Schwimmpanzer II. Its typical feature were floatation/dinghy boxes with propellers power by the tank's engine, mounted on both sides of the Pz.Kpfw. II and delievered to the crossing point on a truck. Such unit could make 10 km/h in the water. The originator of this solution was the Käsbohrer enterprise of Ulm and the contractor – Sachsenberg Brothers' factory in Roslau. According to the research of

Field graveyard of Pz.Kpfw. II Ausf. C tanks, probably somewhere in the rear of the French campaign frontline, late spring 1940. Note details of the driving sprocket mounting in the vehicle in the foreground [Kagero Archive].

Column of Pz.Kpfw. II Ausf. A-C of an unknown Panzerwaffe unit, the first days of Operation Barbarossa; eastern front, summer 1941. At the beginning of the invasion on the Soviet Union there were 1074 tanks of that type in the ranks of Wehrmacht. 746 of them had been sent into combat [Kagero Archive].

the German armoured vehicles expert, Thomas Jentz, prior to the Operation Sea Lion, that is the invasion on the British Isles which in the end was never carried out, the Germans produced 52 sets of such floatation-dinghy boxes. They were all dispatched to 18th Armoured Regiment, consisting of two battalions – Panzer-Abteilung A and Panzer-Abteilung B and beginning with October 1940 they were tested on the Putlos testing ground. Schwimmpanzer II tanks were used in combat only once, on 22nd June 1941, during crossing of the German-Soviet border on the Bug River, in the first hours of the Operation Barbarossa.

The experience of the crews using the second group of the Panzerwaffe light tanks, gained during campaigns in Poland, Scandinavia and Western Europe lay at the heart of the next modernization series of the presented vehicle group. In the view of decision-makers in Berlin, as well as of the crews operating these vehicles, this tank became essential and crucial for the army, especially when the spectre of the large-scale strike on the Soviet Union appeared on the horizon. The production of the Pz.Kpfw. II Ausf. F was planned to begin already in 1940, however due to economical reasons the first vehicles of that type were finished in March, next year. Manufacturing of this type, which totalled to 524 machines (hull number plates 28001 – 28834), was entrusted only to the FAMO factory in Wrocław. It used the components delievered by other factories, including Vereinigten Maschinenfabrik Warschau, that is the State-owned Engineering Plant in Czechowice near Warsaw.

The main changes applied to the hull, which originally rounded glacis plate was replaced with a straight one, 35 mm thick. The driver's and radio operator's positions were protected with 30 mm thick plate, same as the front, the sides and the back of the turret. The driver had a wide visor at his disposal, which was covered with ballistic glass that was not 12 mm thick,

Group of Pz.Kpfw. II Ausf. C during the Wehrmacht victory parade in Warsaw, 5th October 1939. Large white Balkenkreuz painted on the turret sides visible [Kagero Archive].

like used in previous versions, but 50 mm thick! It is probable that glasses of that type were used already in late versions of the Ausf. C model. Bearing in mind that the commander faced much problems while observing the battlefield, the designers decided to mount on the turret a short, small cupola equipped with eight periscopes. The commander could examine the area around the tank without putting his nose out of the turret. Such solution resulted in the necessity to install a new, one-piece, round hatch (the previous model was rectangular and two-part, opening aside). Beginning with October 1940, this modification was introduced to the previous versions of Ausf. A – Ausf. C undergoing repairs and overhauling. In the same time, the toughened, so-called conical idler wheel was installed as well. Some of the Pz.Kpfw II Ausf. F were armed with the more up-to-date variant of the 20 mm gun – the Kampfwagenkanone 38, 2246 mm long. The weight of this version exceeded 9500 kg.

On 20th June 1942, when it came clear that the discussed group of the German light tanks was not able to face the fight-

Concentration of armored vehicles belonging, probably, to 5th Panzer Division, the first days of the Polish campaign, September 1939. In the foreground there are light tanks Pz.Kpfw. II Ausf. C, with characteristic tactical signs painted on the turret sides [Kagero Archive].

Pz.Kpfw. I Ausf. B and Pz.Kpfw. II Ausf. A-C photographed probably just after the end of the French campaign, summer of 1940. The characteristic details of the chassis, installed in Ausf. A-C and Ausf. F variants [Kagero Archive].

ing vehicles of the Third Reich enemies, the headquarters made a decision that half of the produced Ausf. F hulls should be used for producing Marder II self-propelled cannons, armed with 7,5 cm Panzerabwehrkanone 40 anti-tank gun. In August of the same year the production of this tank version was fully suspended. The last 5 vehicles manufactured accordingly with the original project, left the shop floors in Wrocław, in December 1942.

Paralell to the development of the basic version of Panzerkampfwagen II, the designers worked on creating a new fighting vehicle, called Schnellpanzer, that is a cruiser tank. Such a machine, which was admitted as a member of the described vehicle group, was labelled as Pz.Kpfw. II Ausf. D (and its only slightly modified developmental version – Ausf. E). The assembly began in May 1938 in the MAN factory and lasted until

A column of Pz.Kpfw. II Ausf. b light tanks belonging to an unknown Panzerwaffe unit during the French campaign, May 1940. Note the smoke grenades launcher installed on the rear armor plates [Bundesarchiv].

A group of Pz.Kpfw. II Ausf. F light tanks charging through the North African desert, probably the beginning of spring 1942. The first vehicles of this variant were sent to Libyan ports in Benghazi and Tripoli in December 1941 (Buhdesarchiv).

the August, next year. 43 vehicles were manufactured and their hulls were numbered from 27001 to 28000.

Distinguishing this variant should not give rise to any difficulties even for those who are only cursorily knowledgeable in technical complexities of the Nazi armoured troops. Its distinctive feature were large, single hull wheels, Christie type, on which, both on the upper and the lower parts, rested the tracks. They were equipped with lubricated, so-called wet linking bolts or hinges. The glacis plate consisted of straight armour plate, 30 mm thick, with two visors: one for the driver and the other for the radio operator. The Maybach HL62TRM petrol engine installed in the rear part was capable to accelerate this 10 ton heavy vehicle to maximum 55 km/s road speed. The Pz.Kpfw II Ausf D and Ausf. E were the first models in which the designers decided to install pre-selective gearbox Maybach Variorex VG 102129H, offering 7 speeds forward and 1 reverse.

Vehicles of such type were used in combat only once, during fighting in Poland in September and October 1939 (they were distributed among Panzer-Abteilung 67, a part of 3rd Light Division and Panzer-Abteilung 33, a part of 4th Light Division).

Covered with a thick layer of dust, a Pz.Kpfw. II Ausf. A-C of an unknown Wehrmacht armored unit, photographed in a Russian village, summer 1941. At the beginning of the Operation Barbarossa, 746 light tanks of this type had been sent to the frontline [Bundesarchiv].

A presentation of one of the German armored units during the annexation of Sudetenland, October 1938. In the foreground there are Pz.Kpfw. I Ausf. A or Ausf. B light tanks, followed by Pz.Kpfw. II Ausf. c and Ausf. A-C in the background [Bundesarchiv].

In March 1940 a decision was made to withdraw them from the front troops and rebuild into self-propelled flamethrowers Panzerkampfwagen II Flamm Sd.Kfz. 122. In the period from January 1940 to March 1942 112 such vehicles were produced, they made their debut in the summer of 1941, on the eastern front and they were used strictly only at this theatre of operations.

Conclusions drawn during and after combat in Poland in 1939 were the basis for creating and designing another version of Panzerkampfwagen II. This time, wanting to grant proper and adequate support for the infantry sub-units charging at enemy fortified positions, on the 22nd December 1939, the Army Weapons Agency issued an order to design a heavily armoured, tracked direct support vehicle. On 19th June 1940 the representatives of the Maschinenfabrik Augsburg-Nürnberg presented to the Wehrmacht decision-makers a prototype of a vehicle called Versuchs-Konstruktion (VK) 1601. This machine, which went down in the history as Pz.Kpfw. II Ausf. J or Pz.Kpfw II neuer Art Verstärkt used a suspension system of Schachtellaufwerk type, drawn up by engineer Kniepkampf. It consisted of single, interleaved road wheels and was powered by 150 HP Maybach HL45P engine. The hull, unlike the almost every other Panzerwaffe tanks, was not made of lower and upper part, joined with heavy rivets or screws but it was casted as a one, integral component. On the sides, in the space between the mudguards there were round hatches for driver and radio operator to crawl inside the tank. The front, plain armour plate was 80 mm thick, side armour – 50 mm and the roof plate – 25 mm. The weight of the vehicle increased to 18 tons and it was armed in identical way as the versions described earlier in the publication. Generally, in the period from April to December 1942, 22 Pz.Kpfw. II Ausf. J were built (hull numbers 150201 – 150222).

According to the source materials, 7 vehicles of said type were sent in 1943 to the 12th Panzer Division, operating on the eastern front. Their fate remains unknown. Apart from all the above described types, in the last year of the war, at least one technical vehicle, a crane, was built, using a turretless hull of Pz.Kpfw. II Ausf. J.

Armoured reconnaissance

The Third Reich was on a constant quest for an effective, light but well armoured and armed recoinnaisance tank, even before the outbreak of the II World War. On 18th June 1938, the MAN and Daimler-Benz AG factories received an order to create a prototype (and after the approval, also a test series) of a tracked reconnaissance vehicle, with Schachtellauffwerk suspension, code-named Versuchs-Konstruktion 901. From April 1941 to February 1942 most likely 12 such tanks were built, bearing name of Pz.Kpfw II Ausf G (sometimes one might stumble upon versions: Ausf. G1, Ausf. G2 and Ausf. G3, indicating three batches) of hull numbers 150001 – 150075.

Apart from the suspension system, consisting of single, interleaved steel road wheels with rubber tires, the vehicle was equipped with Maybach HL45P engine but its hull was taken from Pz.Kpfw II Ausf. F, although without large driver's visor (a periscope was installed instead). In the turret mounted precisely in the middle, there was not 20 mm KwK 30 or KwK 38 cannon installed but a Mauser Einheitswaffen 141 7,92 mm machine gun, with Tzielfernrohr 10 sights.

What is really curious, the vehicle, weigting 10,5 tons, was to be transported on board of Me-321 Gigant heavy gliders. If this thesis turns out to be true, Pz.Kpfw. II Ausf. G would be the first, and at the same time the only Wehrmacht tank, which redeployment would have been done by air utimately. The High Command of the Ground Forces – Oberkommando des Heeres – wanted to test this property during the planned landing on Malta. The operation did not come off and the presented version never went beyond the test phase.

In August 1942 the army returned to the concept of a light reconnaissance tank (as well as to light observation vehicle in sub-units of self-propelled guns), what was connected directly to war experiences gathered during the first autumn and winter on the eastern front. Drafts and sketches of the VK901 were taken out of the archives and once again placed on the drawing desks, making a basis of the VK903 vehicle, that is the future Pz.Kpfw. II Ausf M. In accordance with the design, the side armour was to be thickened to 20 mm, compared to 15 mm of its precursor and the serial tanks were to be equipped with SSG48 gearbox, taken from Pz.Kpfw. 38(t) neuer Art. It was assumed that a vehicle powered with 200 HP Maybach HL66P engine (6754 ccm displacement) should accelerate to 60 or 65 km/h of road speed (37-40 mph). Finally – and presumably too – the MAN factory in Nuremberg produced only one prototype in September 1942.

Approximately in this period, the same factory completed other 4 experimental tanks, designed for reconnaissance squadrons, the VK1301, that is Pz.Kpfw II Ausf. H (hull numbers from 200001 to 200004). This vehicle might be taken as a developmental version of Ausf. G variant, equipped with larger, open-topped turret, that might be covered with tarpaulin sheet. It was armed with the Kampfwagenkanone 39/1 L/60 gun, calibre 50 mm. The fate of these vehicles was not investigated so far, although it is known that within so-called Armour Programme, in a year or two the armoured units on all the fronts were to receive 13000 vehicles of both described types. For the obvious reasons, fulfilling such a plan was absolutely impossible.

Talking about the history of reconnaissance tanks, belonging to the Panzerkampfwagen II group, one shall recall another,

The Germans greeting the Wehrmacht armored platoon entering one of the Sudetenland cities during the annexation of this area in October 1938. This column is led by Pz.Kpfw. II Ausf. c with characteristic, rounded front hull plate [Bundesarchiv].

very curious structure, which finally never reached the phase of series production. In the spring of 1942, designers in the MIAG plant came up with an idea to build a heavily armoured, fast tracked vehicle, which was named **Gefechts-Aufklärer Leopard** VK1602. Construction of the prototype took place between 30th June and 1st September the same year, what might have granted the Braunschweig factory an opportunity to built the initial series of 105 vehicles, with additional 45 possible. Typical feature of this version was, apart from Kniepkampf suspension system, a fully sloped frontal armour and a little, full turret, armed with 50 mm cannon, identical as in Pz.Kpfw II Ausf. H (turrets of that type were later mounted also on armoured cars Sd.Kfz. 234/2 Puma). The vehicle weighted 22 tons and could reach maximum 60 km/h (37 mph) road speed, thanks to a V-type, 550 HP Maybach HL157 engine (15580 ccm displacement). According to the design, the crew was protected with hull armour plates that were 60 mm thick, while the turret armour reached 80 mm of thickness.

At the same time, the Daimler-Benz factory located in Berlin proposed its own reconnaissance tank, code-named Versuchs-Konstruktion 2801, that weighted 33 tons. This vehicle was to be powered by 525 HP diesel engine or 450 HP petrol engine DB819, alternatively a Maybach HL230 engine (700 HP). Other proposals were put forward by the engineers of Škoda factory (located in Pilzno) and a group gathered around engineer Ferdinand Porsche, who was highly esteemed by the Führer himself. Today, all we know is that none of this projects was granted a chance of series production – all of the experimental programmes in this scope were in the end cancelled on 8th May 1944.

In the spring or early in the summer 1939, in Maschinenfabrik Augsburg-Nürnberg began the story of one of the most characteristic armoured fighting vehicle of the II World War, which was also an absolutely separate chapter in the history of the Panzerkampfwagen II family. The tender for a vehicle VK1303, later renamed into Pz.Kpfw II Ausf L Luchs Sd.Kfz. 123, was attended also by Škoda factory of Pilzno and Böhmische Mährische Maschinenfabrik (BMM) of Prague. Construction of the turret was given to the Daimler-Benz AG company. The essential guidelines for the planned machine covered: the ability to move on adverse terrain, efficiency in severe weather conditions (typical for the eastern front) as well as the immunity to shelling with 14,5 mm armour-piercing rifles and, at a greater range, also to bullets fired from guns of at least 45 mm calibre. The prototype of the "Lynx", which was the final German name for the last, serial version of the Panzerkampfwagen II tank, was ready in April 1942. Even though it was made of, so called, mild steel and weighted around 13 tons, what was took as definitely too much (in the end the weight of Pz.Kpfw II Ausf L did not exceed 12 tons). Although it was assumed that the series production would have been launched in the summer 1943 to produce 800 tanks of that type (700 were to be armed with 50 mm cannon), it was delayed for almost a year. Beforehand, from June to autumn 1942 in Kummersdorf training ground, the VK1303 and rival vehicles of Škoda T-15 and Pz.Kpfw. 38 (t) neuer Art made by BMW were put through a series of exhaustive tests. The MAN prototype, after covering 2500 km altogether, emerged victorious of the trials and it was it which ended up in series production that began in August 1943. Till January the Nuremberg factory made 100 or 123 (18 of which were to be completed by Henschl factory) Pz.Kpfw II Ausf L., hull numbers between 200101 to 200200.

Just like the previous variants of reconnaissance tanks of the Panzerkampfwagen II family, the Ausf. L had suspension system with interleaved road wheels designed by engineer Kniepkampf. The appropriate mobility in cross country was supposed to be granted by 360 mm wide trakcs. The protection of, this time, four person crew was granted by 30 mm armour in the front, 20 mm in the sides and optionally by additional armour plates 12 mm thick. The vehicle was powered by the in-line Maybach HL66P engine, 200 HP and 6754 ccm displacement, granting

The Germans greeting the Wehrmacht armored platoon entering one of the Sudetenland cities during the annexation of this area in October 1938. This column is led by Pz.Kpfw. II Ausf. c with characteristic, rounded front hull plate [Bundesarchiv].

Production of Pz.Kpfw. II, including hull numbers

Tank variant	Hull numbers	Amount	Production period
Pz.Kpfw. II Ausf. a1	20001–20075	25	May 1936 – February 1937
Pz.Kpfw. II Ausf. a2		25	
Pz.Kpfw. II Ausf. a3		25	
Pz.Kpfw. II Ausf. b	21001–21025	25	February 1937 – March 1937
Pz.Kpfw. II Ausf. c		25	March 1937 – June 1937
Pz.Kpfw. II Ausf. A	21101–27000	1113	June 1937 – December 1937
Pz.Kpfw. II Ausf. B			December 1937 – June 1938
Pz.Kpfw. II Ausf. C			June 1938 r. – April 1940 r.
Pz.Kpfw. II Ausf. D	27001–28000	43	May 1938 r. – August 1939 r.
Pz.Kpfw. II Ausf. E			
Pz.Kpfw. II Ausf. F	28001–28834	524	March 1941 – December 1942
Pz.Kpfw. II Ausf. G	150001–150075	12	June 1941 – February 1942
Pz.Kpfw. II Ausf. H	200001–200004	4	August 1942 – September 1942
Pz.Kpfw. II Ausf. J	150201–150222	22	April 1942 – December 1942
Pz.Kpfw. II Ausf. M	?	1	September 1942 r.
Pz.Kpfw. II Ausf. L	200101–200200	100 or 123	August 1943 – January 1944
Gef.-Aufkl. Leopard	?	1	September 1942 r.

Basic Maybach engines for Pz.Kpfw. II tanks – characteristics

Engine model	HL57TR	HL62TR	HL62TRM	HL66P	HL157
Cylinder layout	in-line	in-line	in-line	in-line	V-type
Cylinder amount	6	6	6	6	12
Engine displacement	5698 ccm	6234 ccm	6234 ccm	6754 ccm	15580 ccm
Power	130 HP	140 HP	140 HP	200 HP	550 HP
Maximum RPM	2600	2600	2600	3200	3500
Piston diameter	100 mm	105 mm	105 mm	105 mm	115 mm
Piston stroke	120 mm	120 mm	120 mm	130 mm	125 mm
Compression ratio	6.3:1	6.5:1	6.5:1	6.5:1	6,5:1

Maximum front armour thickness for every Pz.Kpfw. II version

Pz.Kpfw. II Ausf. a	13 mm	Pz.Kpfw. II Ausf. F	30 mm
Pz.Kpfw II Ausf. b	13 mm	Pz.Kpfw. II Ausf. G	30 mm
Pz.Kpfw II Ausf c	14.5 mm	Pz.Kpfw II Ausf. H	30 mm
Pz.Kpfw. II Ausf. A	14.5 mm	Pz.Kpfw II Ausf J	80 mm
Pz.Kpfw. II Ausf. B	14.5 mm	Pz.Kpfw. II Ausf. M	30 mm
Pz.Kpfw. II Ausf. C	14.5 mm	Pz.Kpfw II Ausf. L	30 mm
Pz.Kpfw. II Ausf. D	30 mm	Gef.-Aufkl. Leopard	60 mm
Pz.Kpfw. II Ausf. E	30 mm		

Maximum cannon mount armour thickness for every Pz.Kpfw. II version II

Pz.Kpfw. II Ausf. a	15 mm	Pz.Kpfw. II Ausf. F	30 mm
Pz.Kpfw II Ausf. b	15 mm	Pz.Kpfw. II Ausf. G	30 mm
Pz.Kpfw II Ausf c	16 mm	Pz.Kpfw II Ausf. H	30 mm
Pz.Kpfw. II Ausf. A	16 mm	Pz.Kpfw II Ausf J	80 mm
Pz.Kpfw. II Ausf. B	16 mm	Pz.Kpfw. II Ausf. M	30 mm
Pz.Kpfw. II Ausf. C	16 mm	Pz.Kpfw II Ausf. L	30 mm
Pz.Kpfw. II Ausf. D	16 mm	Gef.-Aufkl. Leopard	80 mm
Pz.Kpfw. II Ausf. E	16 mm		

Maximum road speed for every Pz.Kpfw. II version

Pz.Kpfw. II Ausf. a	40 km/h (25 mph)	Pz.Kpfw. II Ausf. F	40 km/h (25 mph)
Pz.Kpfw. II Ausf. b	40 km/h (25 mph)	Pz.Kpfw. II Ausf. G	50 km/h
Pz.Kpfw. II Ausf. c	40 km/h (25 mph)	Pz.Kpfw. II Ausf. H	60 km/h (37 mph) or 65 km/h (40 mph)
Pz.Kpfw. II Ausf. A	40 km/h (25 mph)	Pz.Kpfw. II Ausf. J	30 km/h
Pz.Kpfw. II Ausf. B	40 km/h (25 mph)	Pz.Kpfw. II Ausf. M	60 km/h (37 mph) or 65 km/h (40 mph)
Pz.Kpfw. II Ausf. C	40 km/h (25 mph)	Pz.Kpfw. II Ausf. L	60 km/h (37 mph)
Pz.Kpfw. II Ausf. D	55 km/h (34 mph)	Gef.-Aufkl. Leopard	60 km/h (37 mph)
Pz.Kpfw. II Ausf. E	55 km/h (34 mph)		

Pz.Kpfw. II Ausf. A-C of an unknown Panzerwaffe unit during the Dutch campaign in May 1940. The 4 return rollers are visible. The poles on the fender were used while driving through a slippery ground [Bundesarchiv].

it maximum road speed of 60 km/h (the driver could use 6 speeds forward and 1 reverse). Probably one testing vehicle was equipped with another powerplant – compression-ignition, V-type, 12 cylinder Tatra engine of 220 HP. The "Lynx" series had 290 km range. The described type had a larger, two-person turret with a quick-firing 2,0 cm KwK 38 cannon, which became standard for later versions of German light tanks, and coaxial machine gun MG 34, calibre 7,92 mm. The main gun had a reserve of 300 shells and the machine gun: 2250. Setting sights on the target was done manually, in range -9° to +18° in the vertical plane. Optical sight Tzielfernrohr 6/38 allowed precise aiming. The vehicle was able to lay smokescreen by itself, using 6 tubular smoke bomb launchers Nebelkerzen 39 9,0 cm, 3 at each side of the turret. The crew did not have to leave the vehicle to fire them (although not all the Luchs tanks were equipped with them). The observation of the battlefield by the commander and the gun layer was granted by two periscopes, turning 360° around. The communication – by two radio sets: Funkgerätsatz 12 (12 km of voice range and 80 km of telegraphic range) and short-range radio Funkgerätsatz Spr. a.

Pz.Kpfw II Ausf L were used mainly for one purpose – as the tracked reconnaissance vehicles. Ultimately every reconnaissance squadron was to be equipped with at least one company of those tanks, although because of limited production capabilities such assumptions were never fulfilled. The main recipient of the "Lynxes" were concentrations fighting against Red Army, mainly the 3rd and 4th Panzer Division and, probably, 5th Panzer Division SS "Viking". On the western front these vehicles were transferred to, most probably, the 2nd Panzer Division, Panzer-Lehr Division and the 116th Panzer Division. 2 Pz.Kpfw II Ausf L tanks belonging to the latter unit fell prey to the Polish 1st Armoured Division during the famous battle of Falaise in August 1944 (battle of Argentan).

Up until today only 2 Luchs tanks survived the test of time. The first one, hull number 200164, which originally belonged to the 116th Panzer Division, can be seen in Bovington Tank Museum (Great Britain), the second one is kept in museum in Saumur (France). Both were captured in summer 1944 by the allied troops fighting in Normandy.

CHAPTER II
Combat employment

In the moment, when the first Panzerkampfwagen II tanks left the assembly lines, it was assumed that they were mainly going to serve as enemy armoured vehicles destroyers and command vehicles at platoon and company level. According with the concept pushed during the 30s. of the 20th century, they were supposed to remain at the front line until the Panzerwaffe managed to equip its sub-units with appropriate amount of heavier, tracked tanks, especially with Pz.Kpfw. III and (then treated as classic support tanks or sometimes called – infantry tanks) Pz.Kpfw. IV. After fulfilling this requisition, Pz.Kpfw. II tanks were to be handed over to training facilities and used for learning.

During the Wehrmacht preparations to the invasion of Poland it turned out that these tanks, in the moment of the outbreak of the armed conflict, would become the prime mover of the Blitzkrieg. That being so, on 1st March 1939 the first unit of light armoured company, adjusted to war-time realities, was issued, in which 15 Pz.Kpfw. II were included: 1 in command section (supported by 2 Pz.Kpfw. I and one command tank Kleiner-Panzerbefehlswagen I), 3 in first, second and third platoon each (along with 2 Pz.Kpfw. I in each) and 5 in the fourth, which was made only by Pz.Kpfw. II tanks. In the same time,

One of the most famous photos taken during the Polish campaign in the first days of September 1939. A Wehrmacht column consisting of, among others, Pz.Kpfw. II Ausf. c or Ausf. A-C light tanks. Every vehicle has a big, white Balkenkreuz, which were later covered with additional paint or mud [Bundesarchiv].

a plan was approved, according to which in eveny tank regiment there should have been 69 light tanks of this version (33 tanks in each battalion and 3 in the command company) and in tank division, depending on its combat use, 84 to 140 machines.

During reorganisation of the German armoured troops, which took place in the first three months of the second year of war, the Pz.Kpfw. II tanks were still included among basic tanks, necessary for the Blitzkrieg strategy. According to guidelines, dated to 22nd February 1940, in one light tank company there should have been 8 tanks of described type: 2 in command section (with 1 Pz.Kpfw. I and 1 Kl.Pz.Bef.Wg. I), and 3 in both first and second platoons (along with 2 Pz.Kpfw. I in each). Third and fourth platoons were supposed to consist only of medium tanks Pz.Kpfw. III. Described vehicles were assigned also to medium tank companies, in teams of 5 vehicles: 1 in command section (supported with 1 Pz.Kpfw. I and 1 Kl.Pz.Bef.Wg. I) and 4 in light platoon (two other platoons of the medium company consisted of 7 Pz.Kpfw. IV each).

Pz.Kpfw. II entered combat on the western front in the arrangement described above. It soon came to light that these vehicles, which less than a year ago prooved efficient in the front line, lost ground in confrontation with British or French tanks – a bullet shot from 2,0 cm KwK 30 cannon, muzzle velocity 800 m/s, went through 35 mm thick, 30° sloped armour from a distance of only 350 meters. This weakness was discerned by army decision-makers, therefore a 2 year period began in which tanks of described types were transferred to reconnaissance units or to special assignment units. According to the Kriegsstärkenach-weisung order (KStN) 171b Behelfs, that was issued on 16th July 1940, a light tank company should have had only 4 Pz.Kpfw. II, assigned only to the command section (the other sub-units were to be reequipped with medium tanks Pz.Kpfw. III and Pz.Kpfw. IV). This amount, among others because of the insufficient amount of the two latter vehicles, on strength of KStN 1171 Sd of 1st February 1941 and KStN 1175 Sd of 1st April same year, the amount of said tanks in both light and medium armoured companies was corrected to 5. Shortly before the German-Soviet war, another order, KStN 6561, saw the light of the day and regulated rules of forming reserve tank companies, in which 3 Pz.Kpfw. II were to make second platoons (what is curious – first platoons should have been made of light tanks Pz.Kpfw. I, at that moment absolutely useless in battle). Apart from that, 5 Pz.Kpfw. II were supposed to be in evey staff company in panzer battalion or regiment (order KStN 1144 Sd of 1st February 1941).

The operation "Barbarossa", that is the Wehrmacht invasion on the Soviet Union, that began on 22nd June 1941, was supposed to turn out as the last huge military venture, in which light tanks, costituing the subject of this publication, were to be used in the front line in a wide and extensive range. The vehicles armed with 20 mm cannons were unable to threaten enemy tracked vehicles at that time and because of that the crews of light Pz.Kpfw. II tanks were assigned the reconnaissance duties (since 1942 in every armoured company there should have been a one reconnaissance platoon of Pz.Kpfw. II) and, more and more, they were also assigned to anti-guerilla operations at the rear of the front. This process intensified in the next years, when the only produced vehicle of that group was Pz.Kpfw. II Ausf. L "Luchs".

Pz.Kpfw. II in combat

The civil war in Spain, that took place in the 30s. of the 20th century, became the testing ground for the armoured weapons of the Third Reich. In the ranks of the Condor Legion, transferred to the Iberian Peninsula, there was the 88th Panzer Battalion, most probably armed in a few or a dozen or so Pz.Kpfw.

Pz.Kpfw. II Ausf. A-C assigned to Panzer-Abteilung 101, the unit which consisted mostly of flamethrower tanks; Operation Barbarossa, USSR, summer 1941. Note the characteristic, white insignia of this Panzerwaffe detachment, painted on the turret [Bundesarchiv].

II Ausf. a, Ausf. b and Ausf. A tanks. One might find mentions and notes on them being used in combat around Ebro River and in Catalonia, in 1939. Another opportunity to test their abilities, especially the mobility of the tracked vehicles, was the Anschluss (annexation) of Austria by the Nazi Germany in 1936 as well as incorporating so-called Sudetenland (1938) and occupation of Czechoslovakia (1939). Although none of these operations was strictly military, the march of Panzerwaffe columns exposed the unreliability of the mechanical system of early Pz.Kpfw. II variants.

The first opportunity to test the presented group of German light tanks was the military conflict with Poland. In the morning of 1st September 1939 1 800 000 Wehrmacht soldiers crossed the eastern border of the Third Reich, beginning the II World War. Since the very beginning of the "White Plan" – the first, military invasion of the Third Reich, the National Army Command had at its disposal 1223 Pz.Kpfw. II tanks of various types. 1151 ended up in the front lines, 67 – in ranks of the Reserve Army (Ersatzheer), deployed all over the country. At that time it was the most numerous vehicle of the German armed forces. Just to show you the numbers: in the war against Poland took part: 1026 Pz.Kpfw. I, 164 Pz.Kpfw. 35(t), 57 Pz.Kpfw. 38(t), 87 Pz.Kpfw. III and 197 Pz.Kpfw. IV. Detailed assignment of Pz.Kpfw. II to infantry divisons and regiments was described in Chart 6.

The light tanks, descibred in this publication, took part in combat already in the first hours of the campaign. On 1st and 2nd September 1939 units of the 1st Panzer Division clashed with soldiers of the Volhynian Cavalry Brigade, near Mokra village near Częstochowa. It turned out that Pz.Kpfw. II was an easy target for Polish crews of 37mm or 75 mm guns – because of that very reason in the first dozen or so hours of fighting already 8 tanks were lost. The next, quite severe losses of these machines were noted by 7th Panzer Regiment, fighting between 1st and 3rd September near Mława: 72 of all 164 tanks in the concentration fell prey to, among others, Polish artillerymen.

The amount of Pz.Kpfw. II in armoured divisions and regiments, taking part in the war against Poland, 1st September 1939.

Division	Regiment	Amount of Pz.Kpfw. II	Division	Regiment	Amount of Pz.Kpfw. II
1.	1.	60	5.	15.	81
	2.	62		31.	63
2.	3.	78	10.	8.	74
	4.	77	Kempf	7.	81
3.	5.	77	1. Light	11.	45
	6.	79		PzA 65	20
	LehrA	20	2. Light	PzA 66	42
4.	35.	64	3. Light	PzA 67	23
	36.	66	4. Light	PzA 33	23

In addition: 58 Pz.Kpfw. II tanks in 25th armoured regiment and 34 Pz.Kpfw. II tanks in I battalion of the 10th armoured regiment, waiting ready in the reserve units.

Many of the tanks lost were indeed Pz.Kpfw. II. These actions were included in the combat log of the I Korps: *the tanks rushed into a barricade, made of railway tracks. This obstacle was not visible in the aerial photographs. Some of them hung on it, becoming an easy target for the enemy. The rest, moving sideways to the enemy line of fire were lost one after another. The attempt to breach the enemy lines was a fiasco. We had to withdraw to the nearest forest, suffering additional losses.*

The crews of the Panzer-Regiment 35 and 36 did no better, but they, along with other parts of 4th Panzer Division, reached Warsaw in the first week of combat. The attack on the capital city, launched on 8th and 9th September from Wola disctrict ended up with 15 Pz.Kpfw. II lost. 4 days before that, at least one Ausf. b vehicle of this unit was lost in the Polish air raid near Radomsko. It is worth mentioning that during the approach to the capital city of the Polish Republic, the 35th

Pz.Kpfw. II Ausf. F belonging to Panzer-Regiment 8 (German 15th Armored Division) during the campaign in North Africa, at the beginning of 1942. Between March 1941 and December next year factories completed 524 tanks of this type. The so called "Rommel's chest" additional stowage box had been installed on the rear plate of the turret [Bundesarchiv].

armoured regiment had only 57 operational of 120 tracked armoured fighting vehicles assigned to it before the war. Photographies depicting Pz.Kpfw. II during this very concentration were taken on the Wolska Street in Warsaw and belong to a group of the most symbolic photographies of the September Campaign.

In the combat lasting till the first days of the October 1939, the enemy managed to destroy 78 Pz.Kpfw. II. On the 1st January 1940, all the Panzerwaffe units consisted of 1010 operational Pz.Kpfw. II tanks, 838 Pz.Kpfw. I tanks, 150 Pz.Kpfw. III and 213 Pz.Kpfw. IV. The participation in the autumn fighting contributed to the notable worsening of the technical conditions of many vehicles, what might be confirmed by a situation that took place in the winter of 1939, in ranks of the 5th Panzer Division. During one of the march of the troops, no fewer than 20 Pz.Kpfw. II broke down in roads and fields of Poland. The reasons of these breakdowns were mainly damages in armour, including cracks of welds in spots where the tanks have been hit earlier, overload of the powerplants and their low resitance to temperatures below zero. The Germans were unable to start 2 of these vehicles, even after delivering them to repair workshops. They were scrapped.

As a part of "Wezera manoeuvres" (Weserübung), which were in fact the armed aggression of the Third Reich on Scandinavian states, on 10th March 1940, the 40th special battalion was created. This unit, being an advance guard of forces invading Denmark and Norway, consisted, among others, of 3 light tank companies, 3 platoons each. Of course, the Pz.Kpfw. II had to be there too. 5 vehicles, along with 12 Pz.Kpfw. I and 1 damaged Pz.Kpfw. IV and 2 command tanks were assigned to the 1st company, supporting the Combat Group Fischer of the 340th Infantry Division. Th 2nd company, which orders were to reach Oslo as soon as possible, had 3 Pz.Kpfw. II (along with 5 Pz.Kpfw. I), supported by a whole platoon, consisting of another Pz.Kpfw. II and 4 Pz.Kpfw. I. The soldiers of the 3rd company, operating along with the 163rd Infanterie Division had at their disposal 6 Pz.Kpfw. II, 5 Pz.Kpfw. I and one command tank.

The clashes with Norwegian and British artillery prooved that the armour of these tanks did not grant sufficient protection for the crews. Luckily, during the whole operation, only 2 tanks of the described types were lost, both during fighting near Gunnlandsdalen, on 15th May 1940. After the end of the operation, the 40th special battalion was assigned to and joined the occupation garrison in Oslo. More Pz.Kpfw. II, that is 18 machines (7 belonging to 1st company, 4 to 2nd company, 5 to 3rd company and one of the armoured platoons Walter and Meier each) appeared. Other vehicles, including 6 Pz.Kpfw. I and one command tank, were transferred to the middle part of the country.

The conquest of Scandinavia marked the first, thorough analysis of the combat effectiveness of the said types of German light tanks. The conclusions were handed to the staff members in Berlin, on 18th July 1940 by the officers of the 40th special battalion and following observations were listed among them: *Taking into consideration situations, in which our soldiers had to operate, it shall be seriously taken into consideration and rethought how to use tanks during assaults on positions manned by enemy anti-tank artillery. Both British and French Hotchkiss guns, calibre 25 mm, had no troubles in dealing losses to our armoured sub-units. The legitimacy of using tanks, including the light ones, in operations in mountainous areas, where changeable and adverse conditions are standard, makes another question. Based on experiences of the crews, one might conclude that the light tanks might be used effectively in combat only when at least one Panzerkampfwagen II leads the vanguard. Its armament, that is main cannon calibre 20 mm, not only allows to reach appropriate and wanted firepower, but also influences the morale of other soldiers taking part in the assault. The combat in Norway prooved the definite superiority of Panzerkampfwagen II tanks over any other light tank we have. They turned out to be efficient in combat against enemy vehicles as well as while using fragmentation-demolishion shells, and in breaching through*

Division	Regiment	Amount of Pz.Kpfw. II
1.	1.	49
	2.	49
2.	3.	55
	4.	60
3.	5.	1
	6.	129
4.	35.	50
	36.	55
5.	15.	61
	31.	59
6.	11.	60
7.	25.	68
8.	10.	58
9.	33.	54
10.	7.	58
	8.	55

The amount of Pz.Kpfw. II in armoured divisions and regiments, taking part in the combat on western front, 10th May 1940.

positions manned only by infantry (...). The effectiveness of this weapon was confirmed in urban combat; the 20 mm shells frequently caused fire of the buildings occupied by the enemy, pushing the enemy troops to flee. These vehicles were also a very good shield for the infantry units, leading the assault.. And although the fire of the guns of said calibre was not as efficient as 75 mm would do, it shall be noted that the KwK 30 cannons, mounted on these vehicles prooved well in combat.

Another campaign, in which the Pz.Kpfw. II of various versions played the key part, was the assault on Belgium, Netherlands, Luxemburg and France. In the moment, when the Wehrmacht began the "Yellow Plan" in May 1940, the combat units had 955 tanks of this group... and the army of the Third Reich had 1100 tanks alltogether. The assignments are detailed in Chart 7. The confrontation with better armoured and better armed machines, which the 3rd Republic Korps had at its disposal at that time, as well as the British Expeditionary Korps, caused the demand to withdraw the Pz.Kpfw. II tanks from the front line appear more and more often. The conclusions of one of the officers of the 35th armoured regiment shall be quoted in here. He wrote about the clash that took place on 14th May 1940, in the Perwez-Malprouve region: *If the Panzerkampfwagen II tanks shall to remain in armed companies, they should be used for specials tasks, like reconnaissance. The alternative is to rearm them with trophy French cannons, calibre 25 mm, that many times proved their worth in combat against tanks. Besides, the observation of the battlefield by the commander should be considerably improved. But back to our ammunition – it proved effective against tanks like Hotchkiss in range of only 200 meters. The thing is that none of our tanks had thickened armour, therefore the crews took great risks in combat like that.*

While completing the Blitzkrieg principles in Western Europe, 240 Pz.Kpfw. II tanks were left on the battlefields. Thomas Jentz established that 194 of them were lost between 10th and 30th May 1940. These losses of Panzerwaffe reached around 35% of the initial number.

The described group of German light tanks operated also in units sent to the Balkan Peninsula. In the spring 1941, 242 Pz.Kpfw. II tanks fought against Greece and Yugoslavia. Just like a year before in Norway, the mountainous terrain and constantly changing weather conditions made the operations much more difficult both for the crews and for the mechanical parts. During the "Marita" and "Kara" operations 13 Panzerkampfwagen II tanks were damaged beyond repairs. Moreover, the 8th and 9th Panzer Division lost additional 5 machines each. It shall be mentioned that 2 Pz.Kpfw. II tanks, originally assigned to the 5th company in the Panzer-Regiment 31, were transported by sea to Crete. These vehicles supported German paratroopers in the Operation "Mercury".

A column of Pz.Kpfw. II Ausf. F light tanks belonging to Deutsches Afrikakorps during maneuvers in Libya, probably in spring 1942. This variant was equipped with redesigned turret; the commander's cupola surrounded with very useful periscopes [Bundesarchiv].

Pz.Kpfw. II Ausf. L Luchs (Lynx) reconnaissance tank belonging to *Panzer-Aufklärungs-Abteilung* 9 of the German 9th Armored Division. It was captured by the Allied forces in summer 1944 and nowadays is exhibited in Tank Museum Bovington [Kagero Archive].

Between 8th and 10th March 1941, the first group of 45 Pz.Kpfw. II, most of the Ausf. C version, assigned to the 5th armoured regiment in the 5th Light Division, were disembarked in Libyan harbour – Trypolis – beginning another series of battles – the campaign in North Africa, which lasted over 2 years. After a parade, which was organised in 12th March, crews headed towards Marsa el Brega, where on the last day of this month they entered combat against British Royal Tank Regiment, armed mainly with cruiser tanks A13 Mk. II. After the battle, the Panzer-Regiment 5 headed through Mechila towards Tobruk. After covering over 700 km, 19 vehicles needed repairs, mainly as a result of engine overheating and mechanical parts gotten too dirty with too much sand.

In the beginning of May 1941, another batch of 45 Pz.Kpfw. II was shipped to the German Afrika Korps, this time assigned to the 8th regiment in the 15th Panzer Division. These vehicles appeared in the front line in the Acromy area. The next 4 machines of the described group were shipped by sea on 30th June. Shortly before the year ended, this time in Benghazi, first 5 Ausf. E tanks were transferred to the North Africa theatre of operations and other 6 were sent to Trypoli. This time, taking into consideration experiences gathered during several months of fighting in deserts, probably all of the vehicles were equipped with a new ventilation system. On 19th December 1941, 32 Pz.Kpfw. II served in the ranks of the Panzer-Regiment 8, which were supported by 68 Pz.Kpfw. I, 16 Pz.Kpfw. IV and 6 command tanks. 14 vehicles of the described type were lost already before the New Years. The balance made before the battle of El Agheila, after 9 months of fighting in the North Africa, was closed with 56 Pz.Kpfw II Ausf C and Ausf. F destroyed or damaged beyond repair.

Upper view of the same vehicle. This photo was probably taken after sending the tank to the United Kingdom [Kagero Archive].

Pz.Kpfw. II Ausf. L Luchs (Lynx) belonging to one of the Wehrmacht armored reconnaissance unit during the fights on the eastern front. The vehicle is coated with, washable paint. Early spring 1944 [Bundesarchiv].

On 5th January 1942 another batch of second-class German light tanks was unloaded in Libya. After 2 weeks only 7 were operational, out of 12 shipped. All of them took part in the decisive German counteroffensive, which pushed the British forces back to Tobruk. Until May of the same year, next 20 Pz.Kpfw. II appeared on the southern shores of the Mediterranean Sea and in June they clashed for the first time with better armoured and armed tanks produced by Americans: M3.

In less than 6 weeks, the allies managed to eliminate 25 Panzerkampfwagen II tanks out of combat; 29 operational tanks left. In the end of the summer 1942 they penetrated British lines in the battle of El Alamein, taking part in the decisive battle in the North African campaign. The last Pz.Kpfw. II tanks left, belonging to 10th Panzer Division, took part in the last fighting of the Africa Army Group, in Tunisia, in the spring of the next year.

The last campaign, in which Pz.Kpfw. II played a major, front-line role was the Operation "Barbarossa", the Wehrmacht invasion on the Soviet Union, which was launched on 22nd June 1941. In this period, 1074 vehicles of various versions of this tank served in the ranks of Panzerwaffe, including a special group of above mentioned Schwimmpanzer II and self-propelled flamethrowers, placed on Ausf. D and Ausf. E chassis. 746 vehicles were deployed in the first attack front line units. Till the end of December, the soldiers of the Red Army managed to eliminate for good 424 of them.

It is worth to emphasise that on the eastern front at least 20 Pz.Kpfw. II fought in ranks of states that entered the military alliance with Third Reich. The states using said tanks were for sure: Bulgaria, Slovakia (Slovakian vehicles appeared on the front line again in 1944, during the national uprising) and Romania. The latter one, already when the II World War was finished, sold some of its tanks to the Lebanese army – their turrets are still present as a part of fortifications at the Golan Heights. Such was the symbolic end of the most numerous German light tank of the II World War.

Pz.Kpfw. II camouflage

The vast majority of the Panzerkampfwagen II light tanks was painted accordigly to the directive issued in 1935, ordering that every German armoured vehicle leaving assembly lines shall be covered uniformly with dark grey paint Panzer Grau RAL 7027. This pattern was reapproved on the strength of Heeres Mitelungen 864 instruction, issued on 31st July 1940. It shall be assumed that vehicles used in 1935-37 period might have been painted with rare, bicolour camouflage, consisting of dark grey undercoat and irrefular dark brown spots, covering around 33% of the outer surface. In winter, the vehicles were painted with white, removable white paint, delivered to the front units in the form of a concentrate or just whitewashed with chalk or lime. Such system was approved officially on 18th November 1941. On the other hand, tanks assigned to fighting in North Africa and, probably, in the southern section of the eastern front, were additionally painted with various shades of yellow, today called Afrikakorps Gelb.

The Pz.Kpfw. II Ausf. L tanks were not painted with dark grey painting pattern but already with camouflage approved in the Directive No. 181 of 18th February 1943. It was explained in the directive, that the base coat for all the armoured vehicles of the Third Reich would be the sand-gray colour – Wehrmacht Olive/Dunkelgelb RAL 7028. Machines prepared in such manner were delivered straight to the front and there, depending on the specifity of tasks, the camouflage was completed with irregular spots or stripes in olive green – Olive Grün RAL 8002 and brown Brun RAL 8017. Frequently, only one of mentioned colours was used to finish the camouflage pattern.

Bibliography

Bischop C., *German Panzers in World War II*, Stroud 2008.
Chamberlain P., *Encyclopedia of German Tanks of World War Two*, London 1994.
Cockle T., *Armor of the Deutsches Afrikakorps*, Hong Kong 2000.
De Sisto F., *Panzer vor! German Armor at War 1939–1945*, Hong Kong 2006.
Feenstra J., Achtung Panzer. *The German Invasion of France and the Low Countries*, Hong Kong 2003.
Guderian H., *Achtung Panzer! Uwaga czołgi!*, Warsaw 2012.
Guderian H., *Wspomnienia żołnierza*, Warsaw 1991.
Jentz T., *Panzertruppen. The Complete Guide to the Creation & Combat Employment of Germany's Tank Force 1939–1942*, Atglen 1996.
Jędrzejewski D., *Niemiecka broń pancerna 1939–1945*, Warsaw 1994.
Ledwoch J., *Panzer II*, Warsaw 1994.
Ledwoch J., *PzKpfw II Luchs Aufklärungspanzer 38(t)*, Warsaw 2000.
Michulec R., *Panzer-Division 1935–1945 (1). The Early Years 1935–1941*, Hong Kong 2000.
Michulec R., *Panzerwaffe at War (1). Nuremberg to Moscow*, Hong Kong 1997.
Keeling C., *Die Kunst der Panzerkampfes*, BDMW.
Manteuffel H. von, *Die 7. Panzer-Division im Zweiten Weltkrieg. Einsatz und Kampf der "Gespenster-Division" 1939–1945*, Cologne 1965.
Perrett B., *Panzerkampfwagen IV Medium Tank 1936–1945*, Oxford 1999.
Pimlott John, *Rommel o sobie*, Poznań 2001.
Ritgen H., The 6th Panzer Division 1937–1945, Oksford BDW.
Scheibert H., *Panzer in Russland. Die deutschen gepanzerten Verbände im Russland-Feldzug 1941–1944*, Dorheim 1971.
Scheibert H., *Panzer II*, Dorheim 1976.
Wijers H., *Od Stalingradu do Berlina. Wspomnienia niemieckich żołnierzy z frontu wschodniego*, Warsaw 2010.

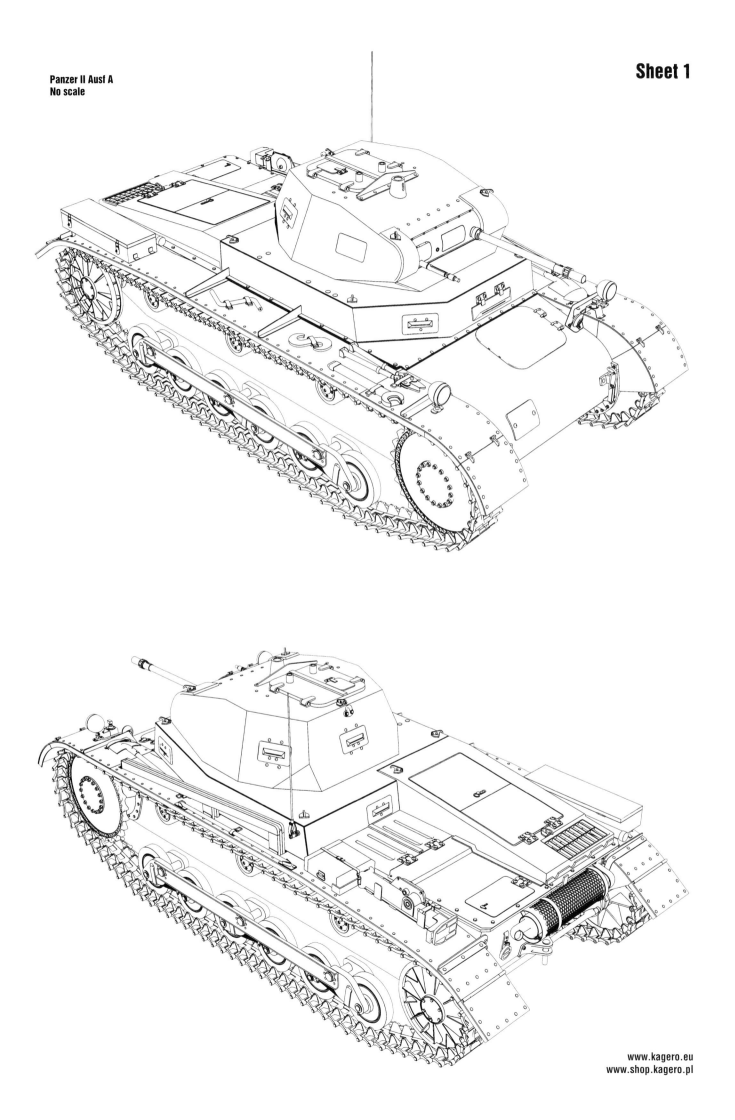

Sheet 2

Panzer II Ausf A
No scale

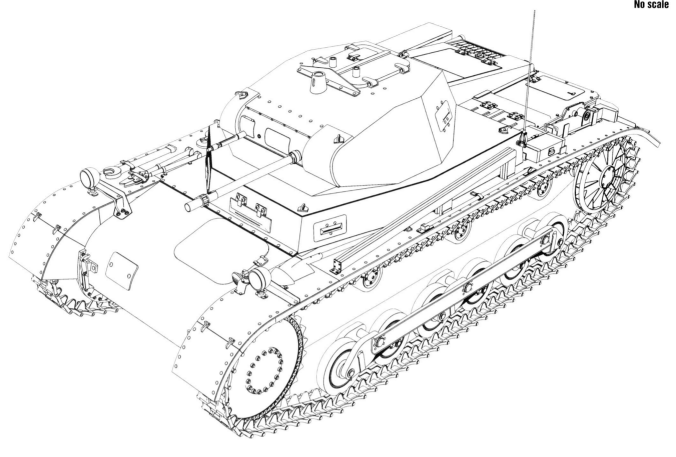

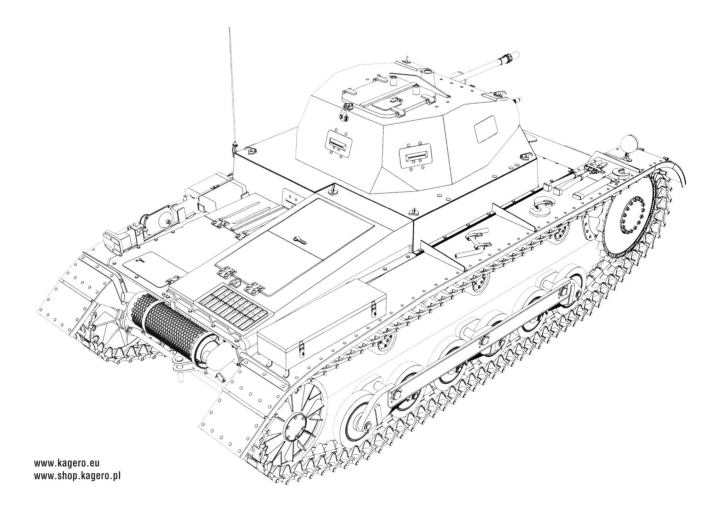

www.kagero.eu
www.shop.kagero.pl

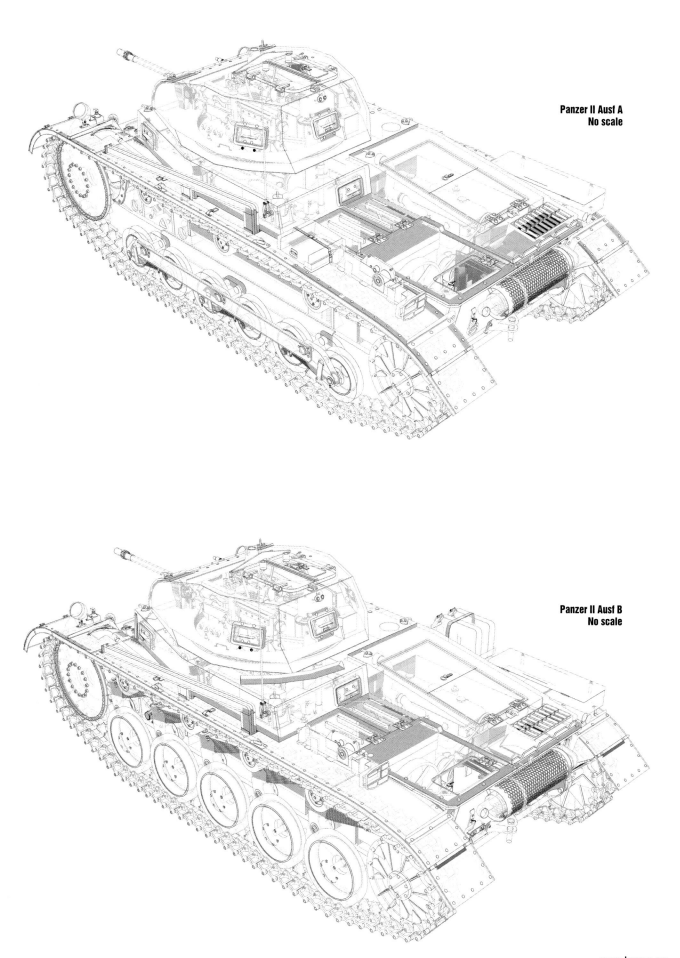

Sheet 4

Panzer II Ausf B
No scale

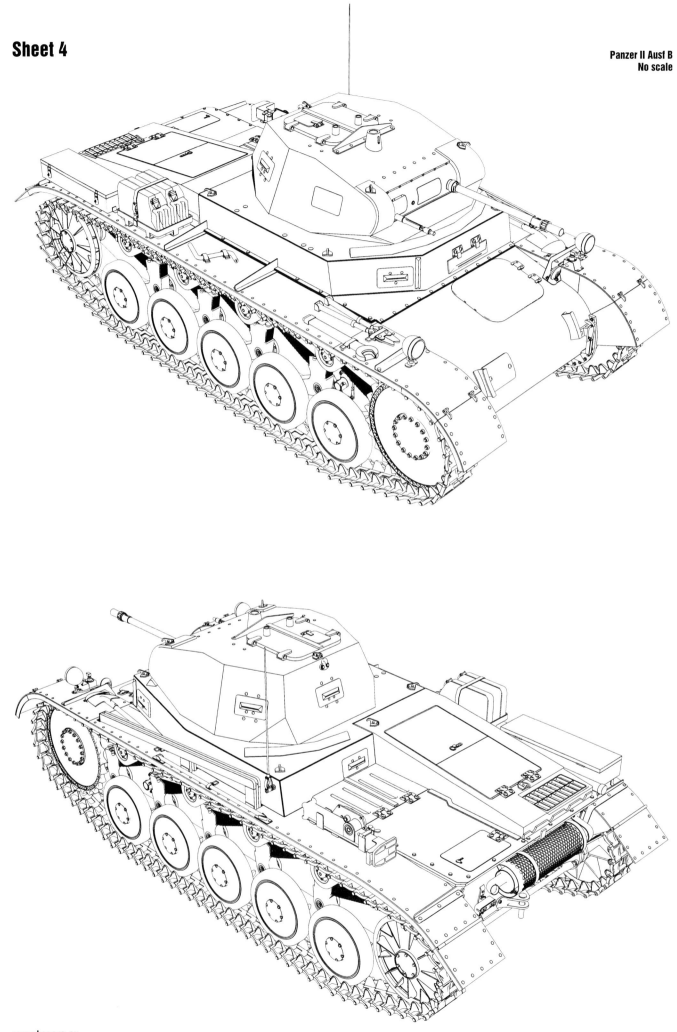

www.kagero.eu
www.shop.kagero.pl

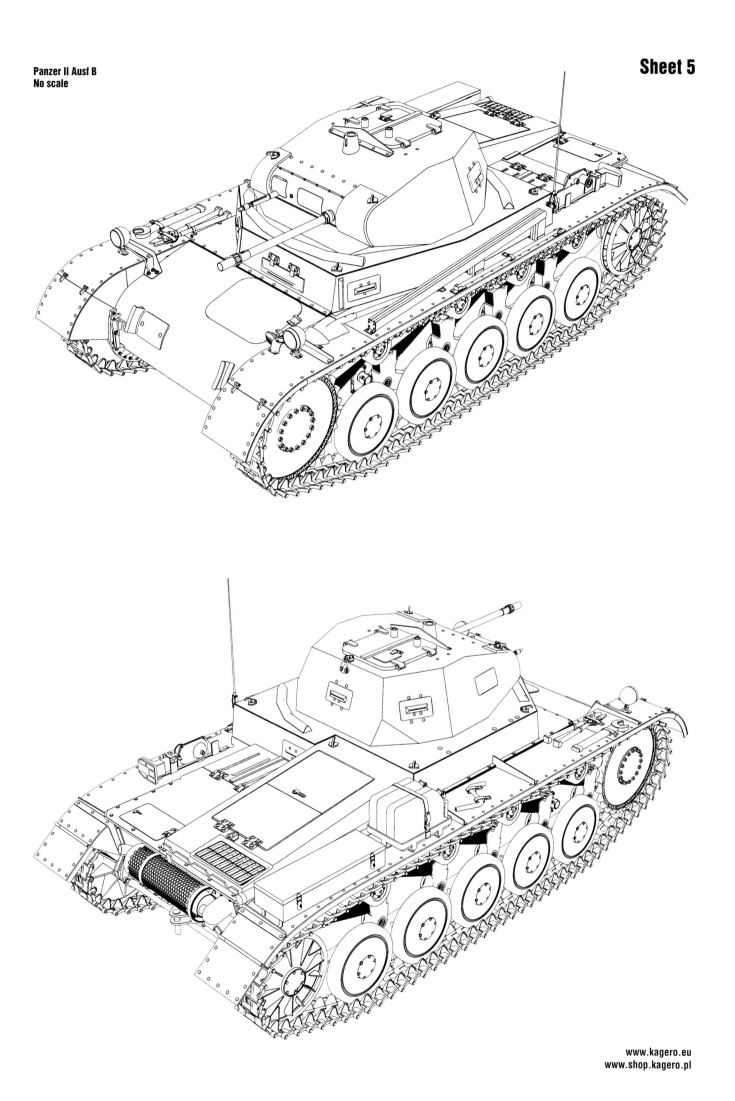

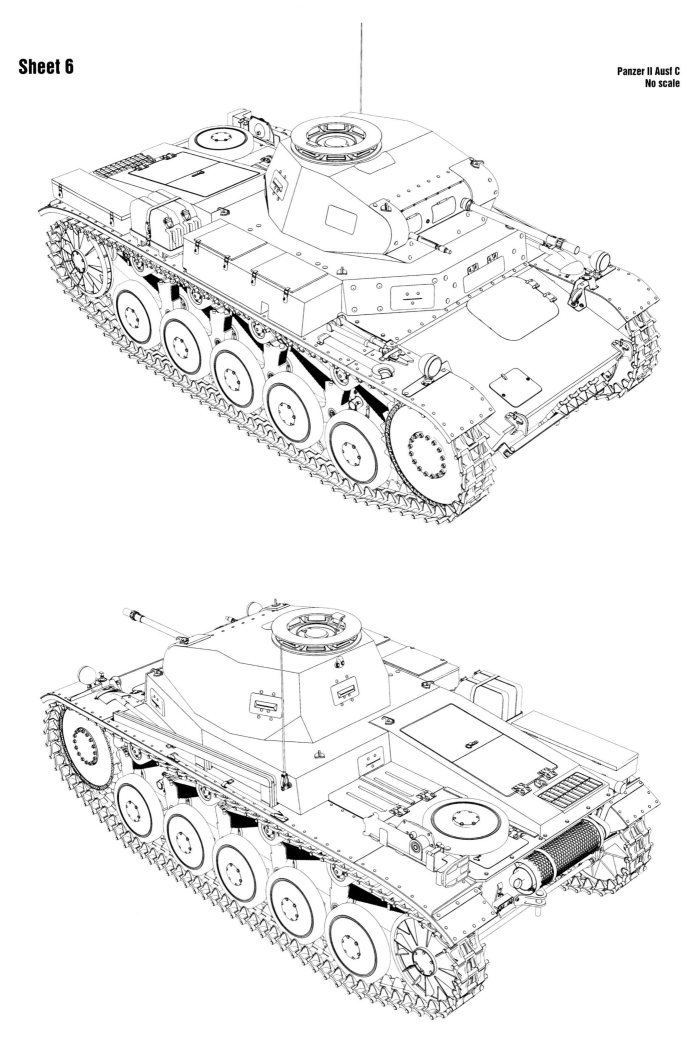

Panzer II Ausf C
No scale

Sheet 7

www.kagero.eu
www.shop.kagero.pl

Sheet 8

Panzer II Ausf C
No scale

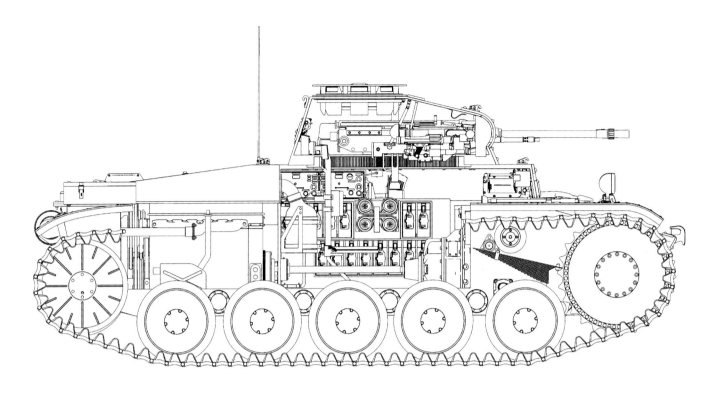

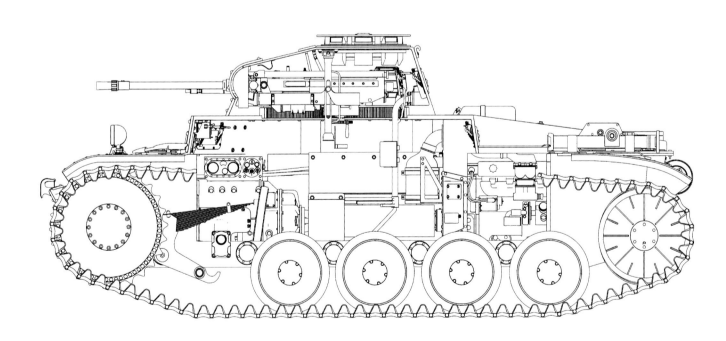

www.kagero.eu
www.shop.kagero.pl

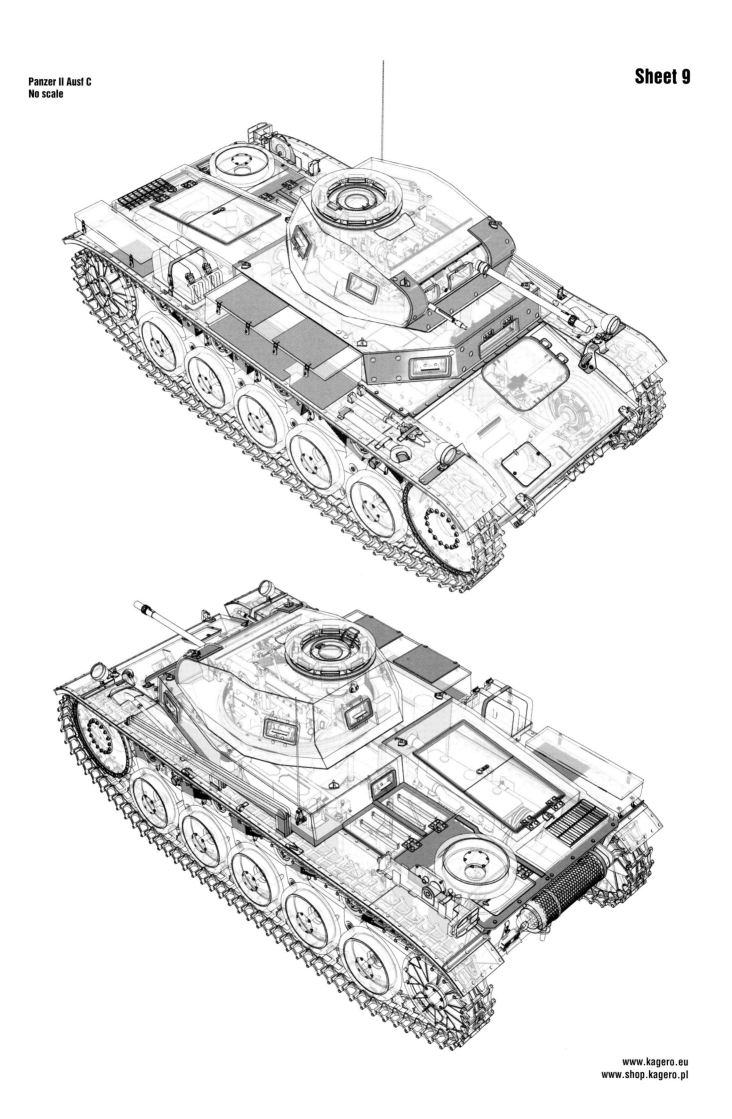

Panzer II Ausf C
No scale

Sheet 9

www.kagero.eu
www.shop.kagero.pl

Sheet 10

Panzer II Ausf D
No scale

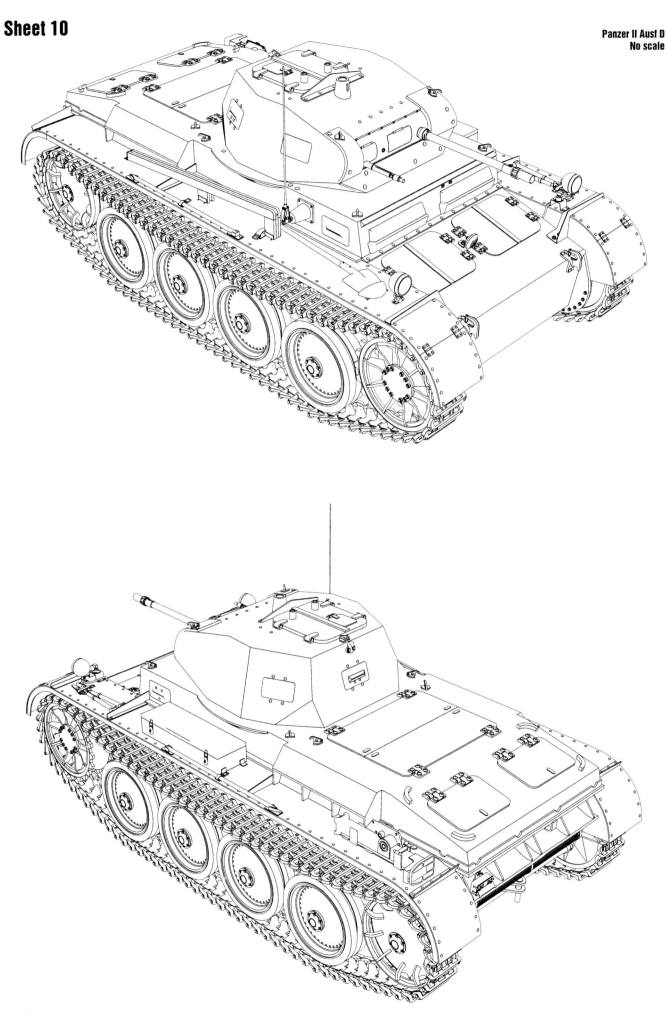

www.kagero.eu
www.shop.kagero.pl

Panzer II Ausf D
No scale

Sheet 11

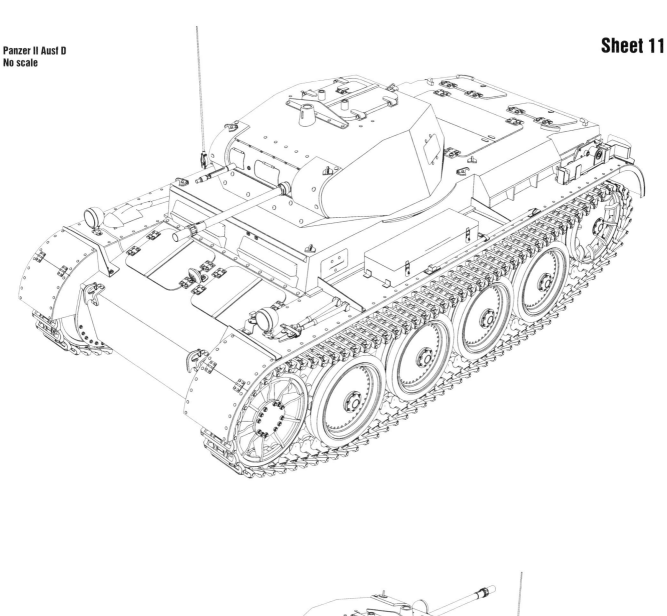

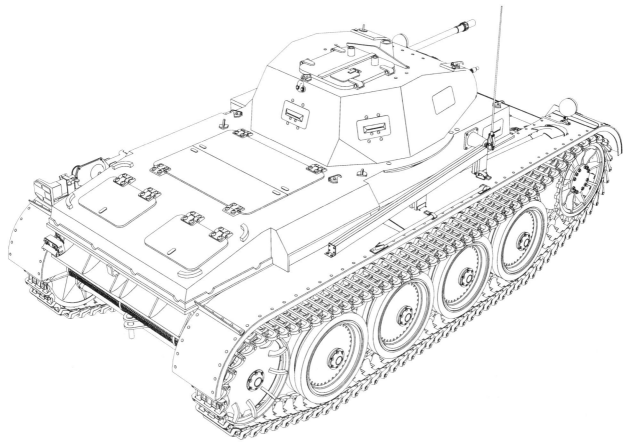

www.kagero.eu
www.shop.kagero.pl

Sheet 12

Panzer II Ausf F
No scale

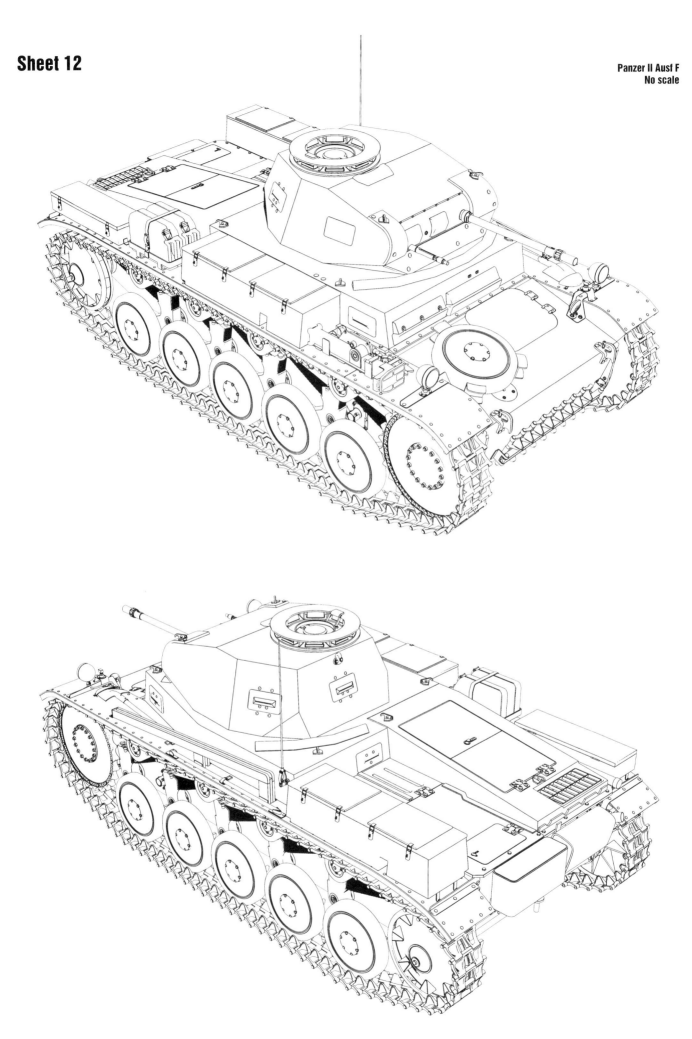

www.kagero.eu
www.shop.kagero.pl

Panzer II Ausf F
No scale

Sheet 13

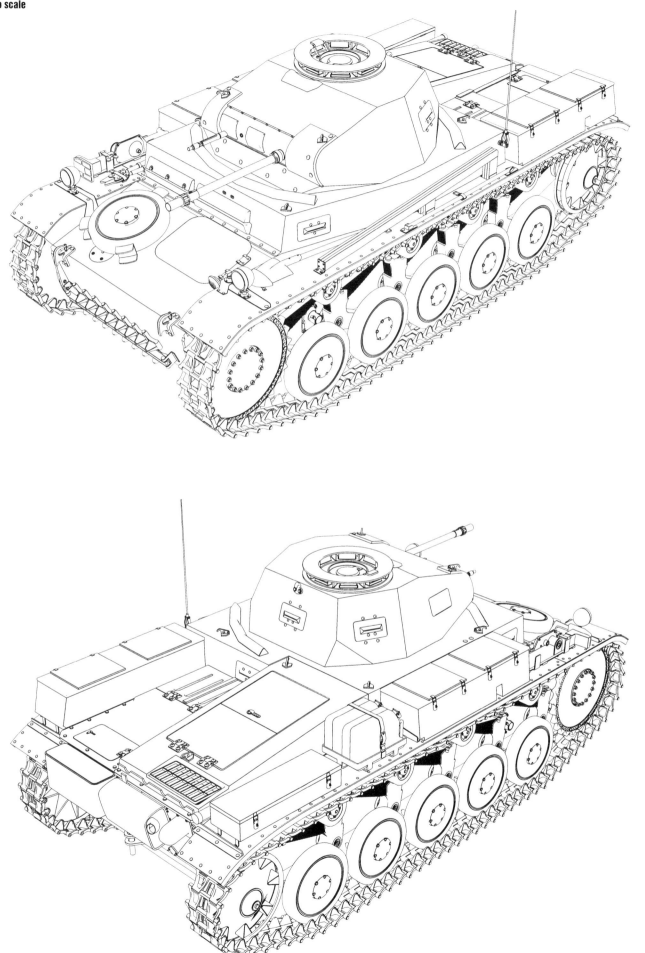

www.kagero.eu
www.shop.kagero.pl

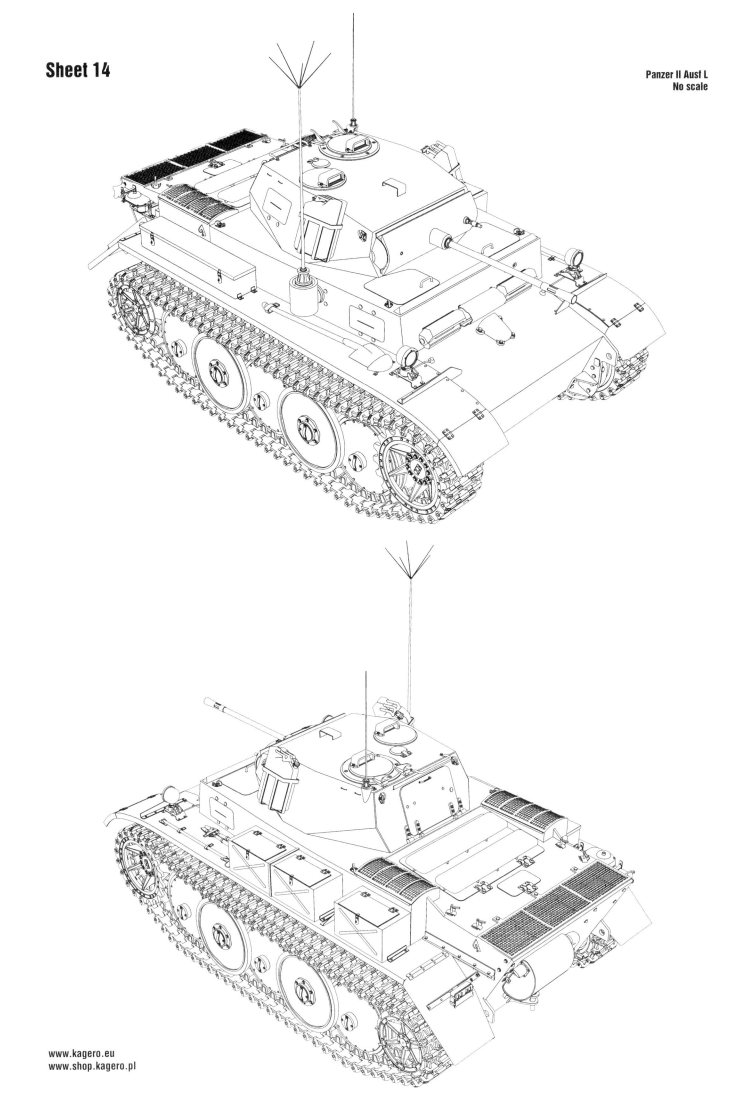

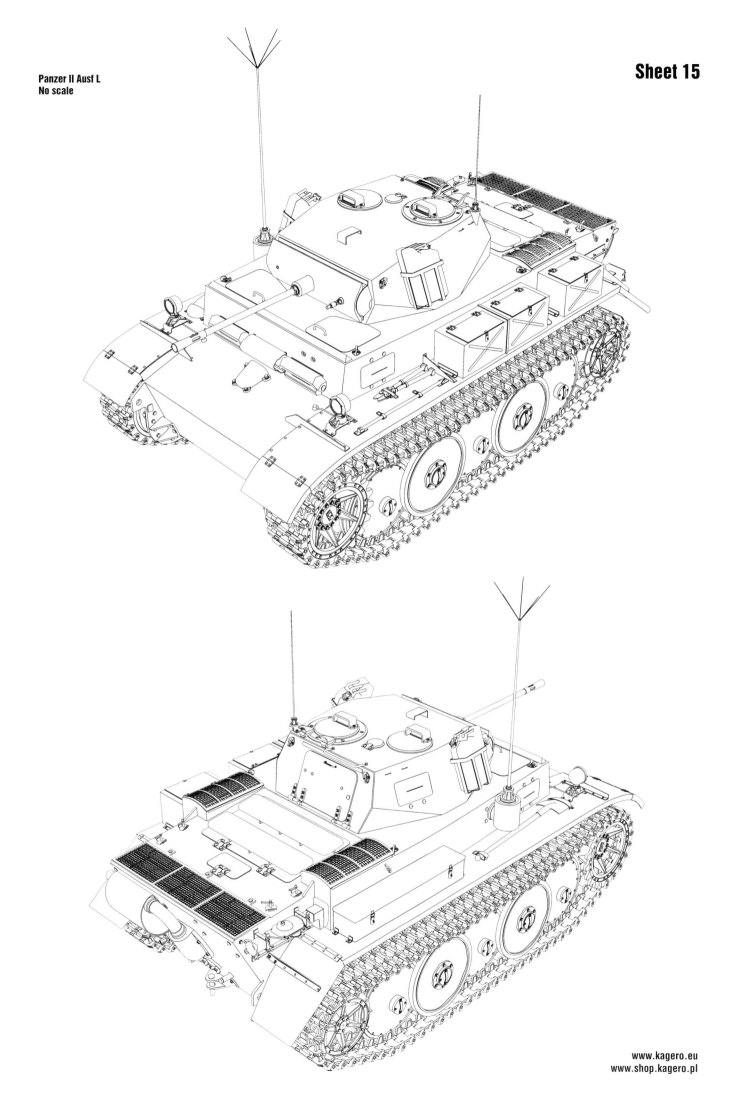

Panzer II Ausf L
No scale

Sheet 15

Painted by Samir Karmieh

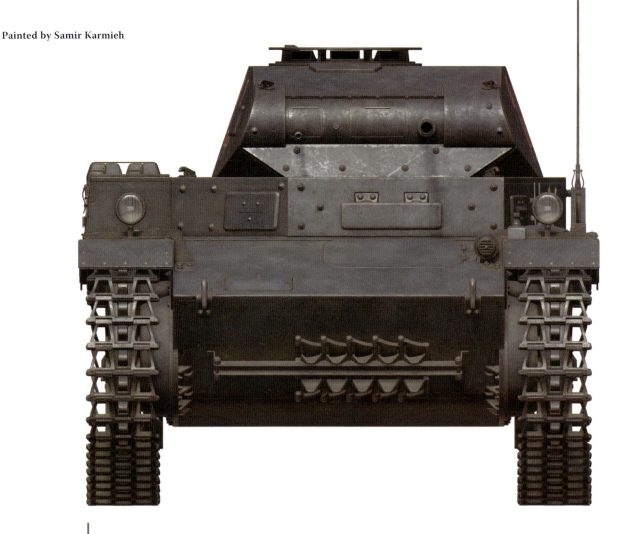

Front and rear view of the late production series *Pz.Kpfw. II Ausf. C* light tank. Major modifications od this model was the straight, weldede hull front part and the commander's cupola installed from autumn 1940.

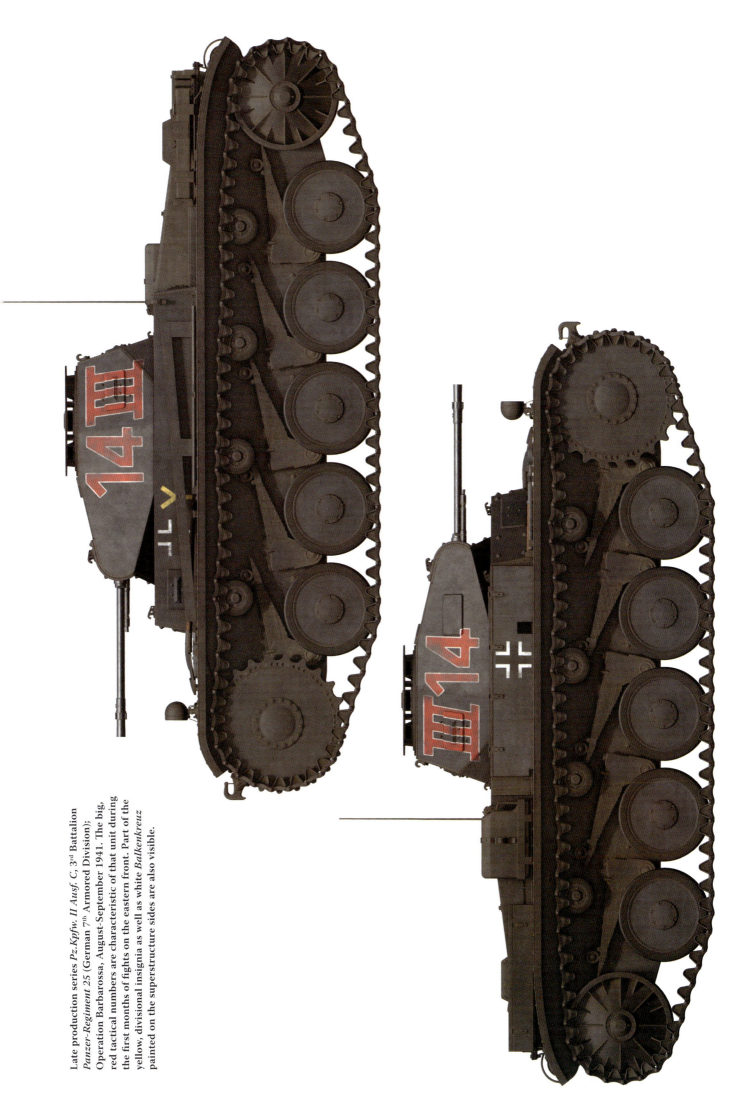

Late production series *Pz.Kpfw. II Ausf. C*, 3rd Battalion *Panzer-Regiment 25* (German 7th Armored Division); Operation Barbarossa, August-September 1941. The big, red tactical numbers are characteristic of that unit during the first months of fights on the eastern front. Part of the yellow, divisional insignia as well as white *Balkenkreuz* painted on the superstructure sides are also visible.

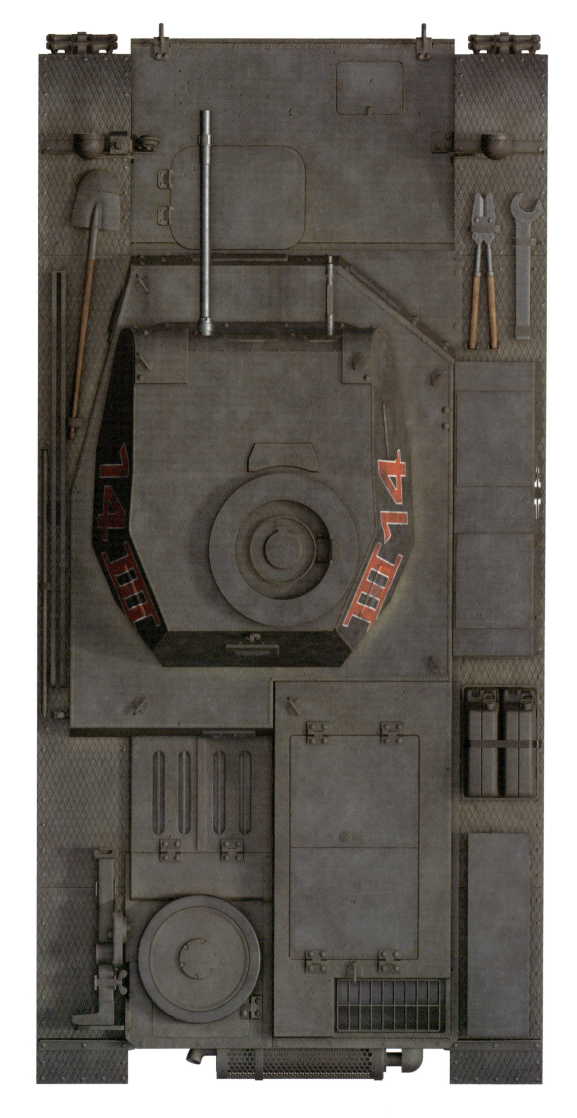

Upper view of the same tank, not the external equipement installed on the fenders and commander's cupola added after the crews' complaints in 1939-1940 period.

Left front corner view of the late production series *Pz.Kpfw. II Ausf. C* belonging to the *Panzer-Regiment 25* in summer 1941.

Right rear corner view of the same tank with a pair of jerry cans, stowage boxes, muffler, jack and spare road wheel clearly visible.

Right front corner view of late production series *Pz.Kpfw. II Ausf. C*. Despite the fact that the hull front had been changed, the superstructure front plate represents the so called early variant.

Left rear corner view of the same tank with the command section of the 3rd Battalion of *Panzer-Regiment 25* big, red insignia visible.

Another views of the same tank. The monotone, Panzer Grau camouflage scheme was characteristic for German military vehicles in the first half of the World War II. In February 1943 the primary color was changed to sand yellow, but in fact this reform was fully implemented not earlier than in spring next year.

The rear plate of the late production series *Pz.Kpfw. II Ausf. C* with muffler, towing hook and *Notek* light.

Details of the left road wheels, return rollers and idler wheel in so called last model dedicated to the *Pz.Kpfw. II* light tanks.

Front part of the late production series *Pz.Kpfw. II Ausf. C* with light made by Bosch and driver's visor.

Exterior view of the driver's compartment left side. Not the visor and a part of the antenna gutter.

In autumn 1940 the commander's cupola with eight periscopes started to be installed. It definitely expand the field of view when the hatch was closed. Another modification were additional armor plates on the turret front.

Right side of the late production series *Pz.Kpfw. II Ausf. C* with the visor cover rised.

Another view of the same tank's turret with commander's cupola clearly visible. Despite the fact that the periscopes had been installed, the turret side visors were still present.

Close up of the *Pz.Kpfw. II* light tanks main armament: was *2,0 cm Kampfwagenkanone 30 L/55* barrel. The coaxial machine gun is clearly visible too. Not the additional armor plates bolted to the front part of superstructure and turret.

Exterior view of the right side of turret and driver's compartment of the late production series *Pz.Kpfw. II Ausf. C* with additional armor plates and part of external equipment.

Another view of the same tank's front part. The visor flaps and armament of the vehicle are clearly visible as well as transmission hatch in front of the driver's compartment.

Right side of the late production series *Pz.Kpfw. II Ausf. C* turret with additional armor and commander's cupola. The last element with its eight periscopes remained unchanged till the end of the World War II.

Details of the commander's cupola and two of the side visors of the same tank.

Bolting the additional armor plates, usually 20 mm thick, was common modification not only of the *Pz.Kpfw. II* tanks. It was the cheaper and faster method that the crew could have felt safer.

There was the additional visor installed on the *Pz.Kpfw. II* light tank superstructure rear visor.

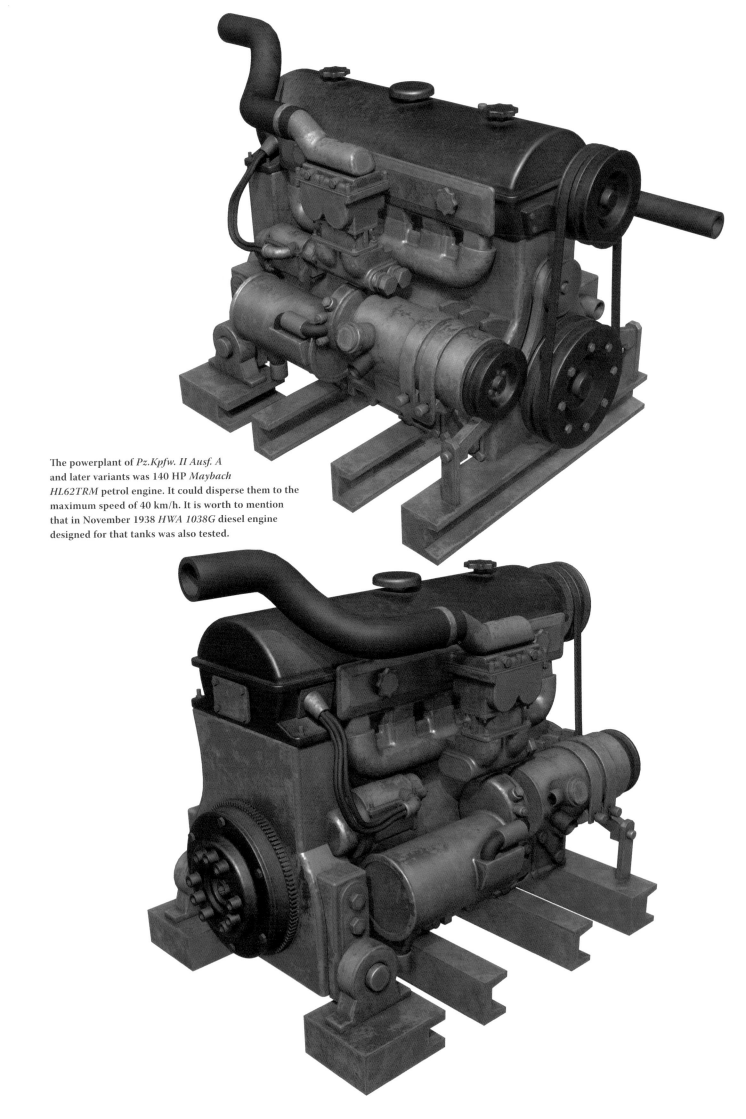

The powerplant of *Pz.Kpfw. II Ausf. A* and later variants was 140 HP *Maybach HL62TRM* petrol engine. It could disperse them to the maximum speed of 40 km/h. It is worth to mention that in November 1938 *HWA 1038G* diesel engine designed for that tanks was also tested.

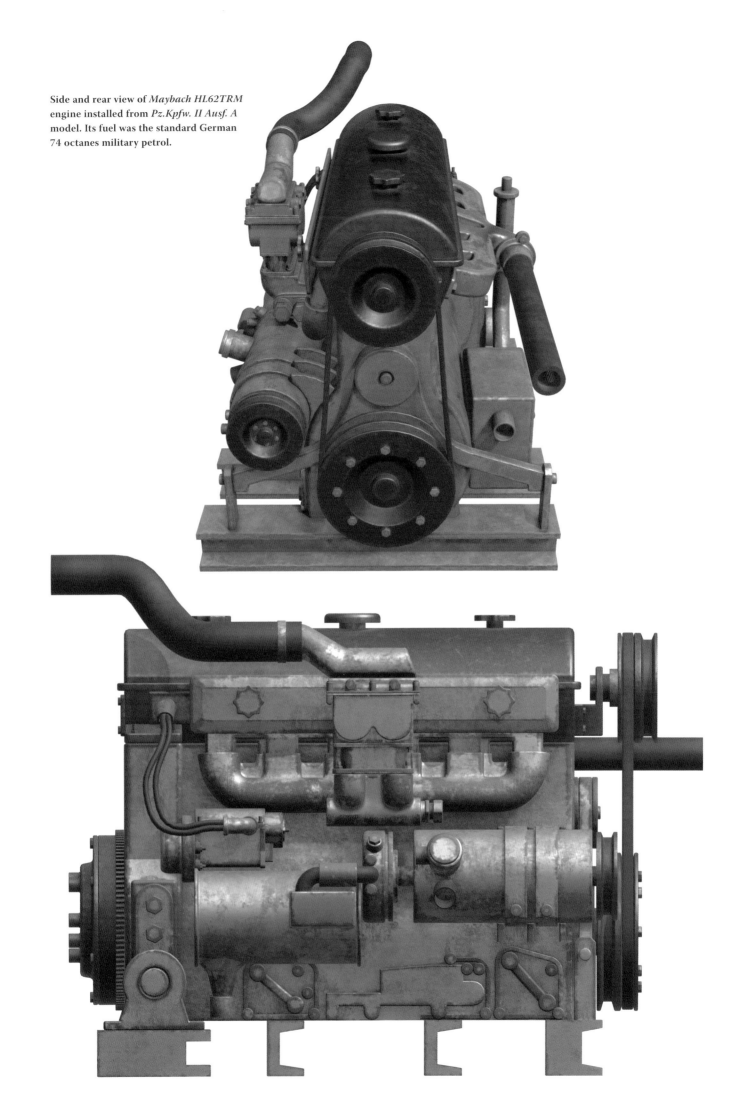

Side and rear view of *Maybach HL62TRM* engine installed from *Pz.Kpfw. II Ausf. A* model. Its fuel was the standard German 74 octanes military petrol.

Another views of the same 140 HP engine.

The driver's compartment and transmission hatch in open position. Some details of the interior are visible too.

Front part of the left side suspension with characteristic driving sprocket, road wheels and return rollers with rubber bandages.

Pz.Kpfw. II Ausf. C idler wheel.

Upper view of the late production series *Pz.Kpfw. II Ausf. C* light tank's engine deck. There was enough space to install the spare road wheel there. The crew often use the deck to transport different extra equipment too.

Every *Panzerwaffe* tank was equipped with a heavy jack. In the case of *Pz.Kpfw. II* it was installed in the rear part of its left fender.

Upper view of the late production series *Pz.Kpfw. II Ausf. C* engine deck with the power plant compartment hatch open.

Cross section of the same tank's driver's compartment with transmission unit.

Funkgerätsatz 12 and *Funkgerätsatz Spr. a* radio set of *Pz.Kpfw. II* light tank.

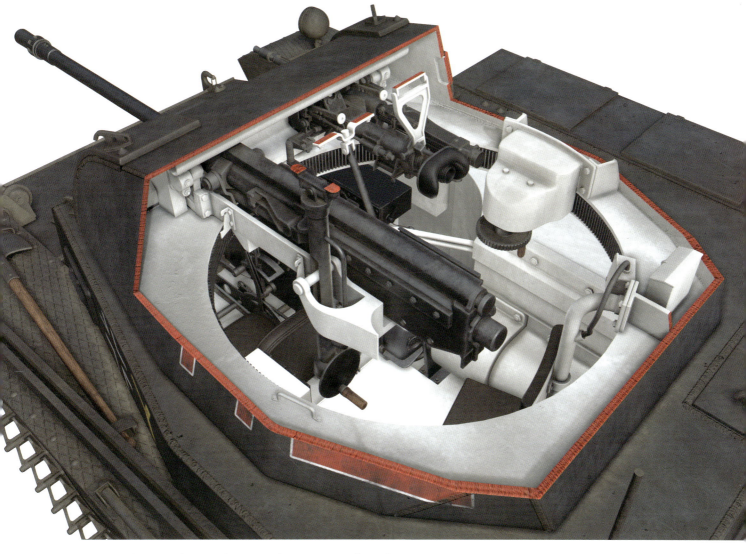

Cross section of the late *Pz.Kpfw. II Ausf. C* turret. The *2,0 cm Kampfwagenkanone 30 L/55* main gun is clearly visible.

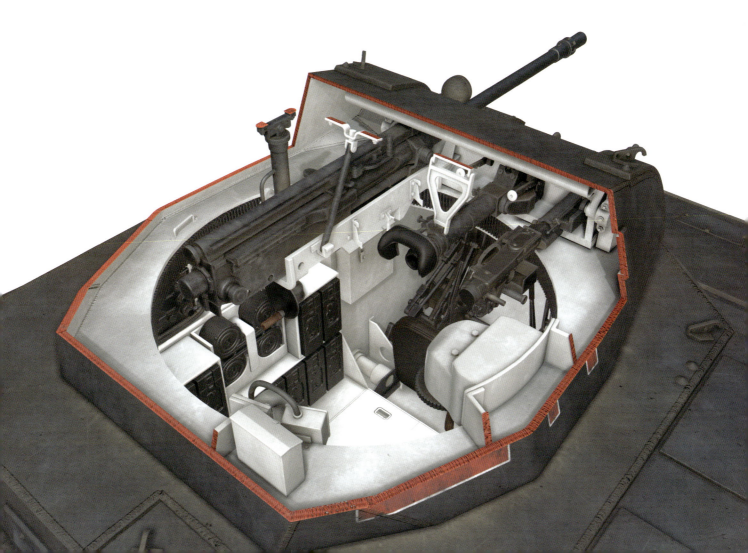

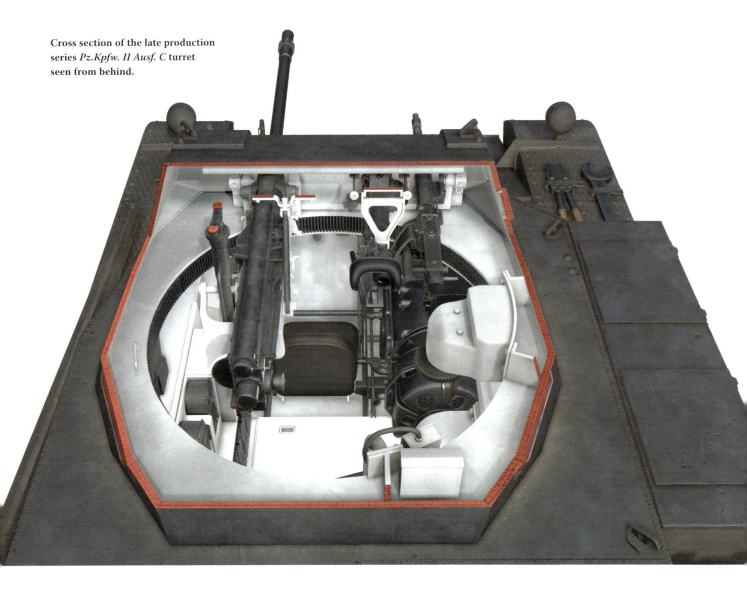

Cross section of the late production series *Pz.Kpfw. II Ausf. C* turret seen from behind.

Left side of the same element.

Upper left view of the same element.

Details of the late version of the *Pz.Kpfw. II Ausf. C* turret interior. The traverse and elevation cranks are clearly visible, as well as *2,0 cm Kampfwagenkanone 30 L/55 massive lock.*

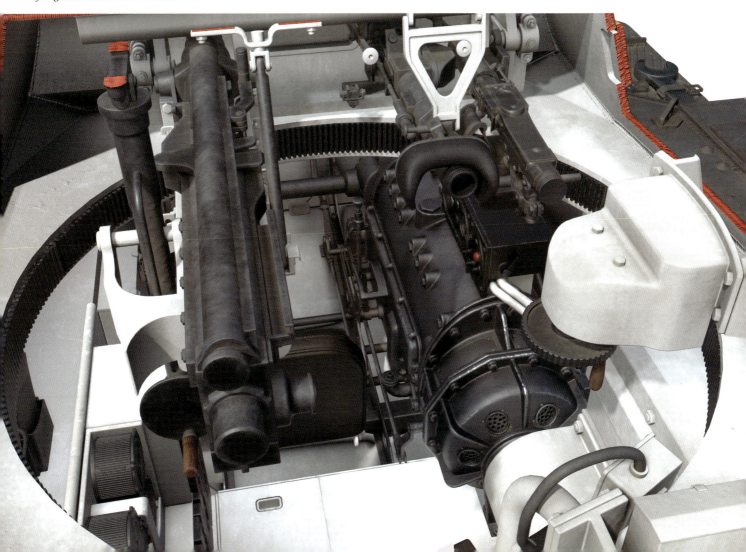

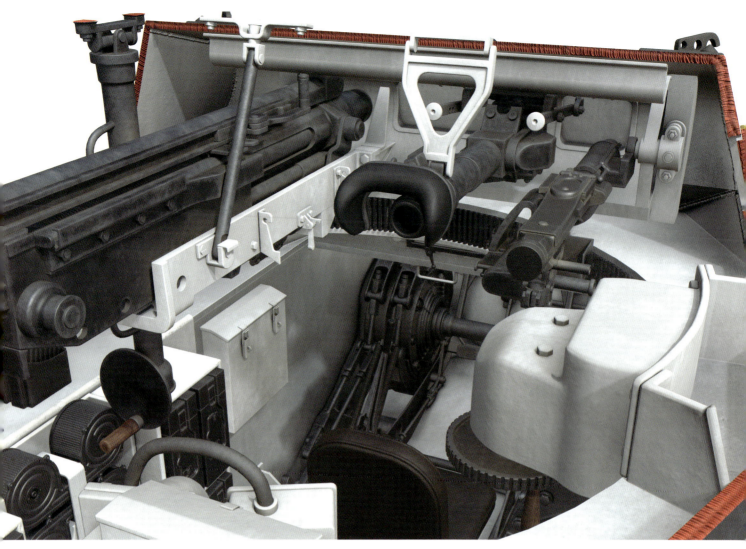

Main armament *Tzielfernrohr 4/38* optical sight and coaxial machine gun installed right to the late *Pz.Kpfw. II Ausf. C* main gun. The ammunition was closed in cases visible in the background of the picture below.

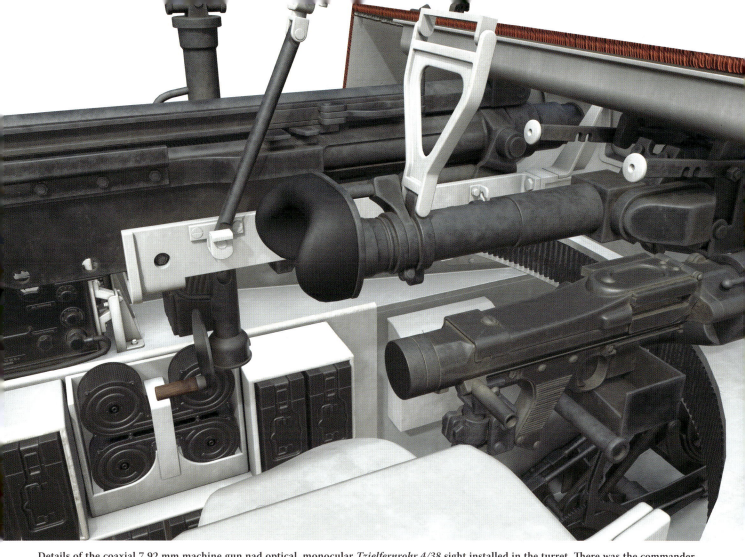

Details of the coaxial 7,92 mm machine gun nad optical, monocular *Tzielfernrohr 4/38* sight installed in the turret. There was the commander, who maintained that devices.

The driver's compartment visible from behind. The transmission block and dashboard are visible on the right.

The field observation by the driver was possible using three visor ports – one on the left, another on the right, and the largest, central one.

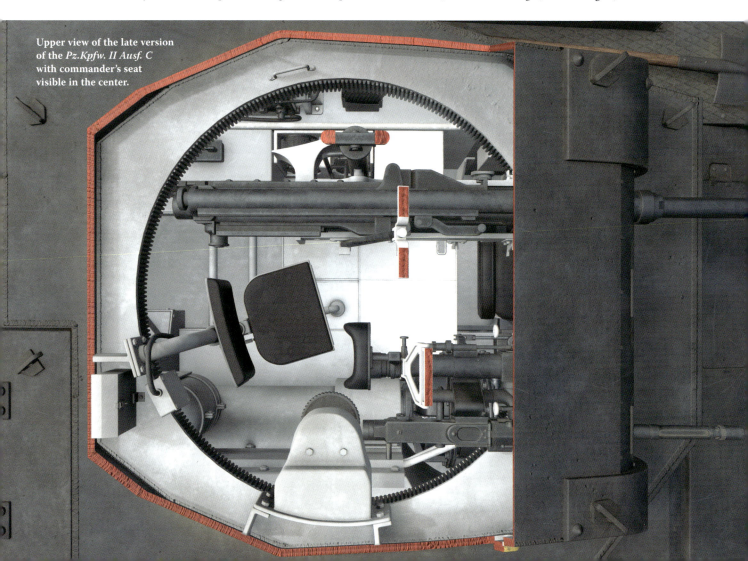

Upper view of the late version of the *Pz.Kpfw. II Ausf. C* with commander's seat visible in the center.

The main armament of Pz.Kpfw. II Ausf. C tank was 2,0 cm Kampfwagenkanone 30 L/55 which was quite similar to the 20 mm Flak 30 anti-aircraft gun.

There were three types of optical sights mounted in Pz.Kpfw. II light tanks. This one represents the Tzielfernrohr 4/38 which was characteristic for Pz.Kpfw. II Ausf. C-F variants.

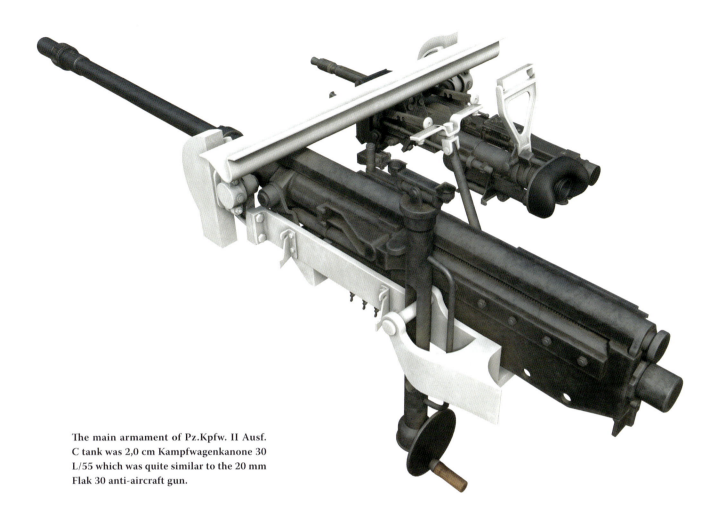

The main armament of Pz.Kpfw. II Ausf. C tank was 2,0 cm Kampfwagenkanone 30 L/55 which was quite similar to the 20 mm Flak 30 anti-aircraft gun.

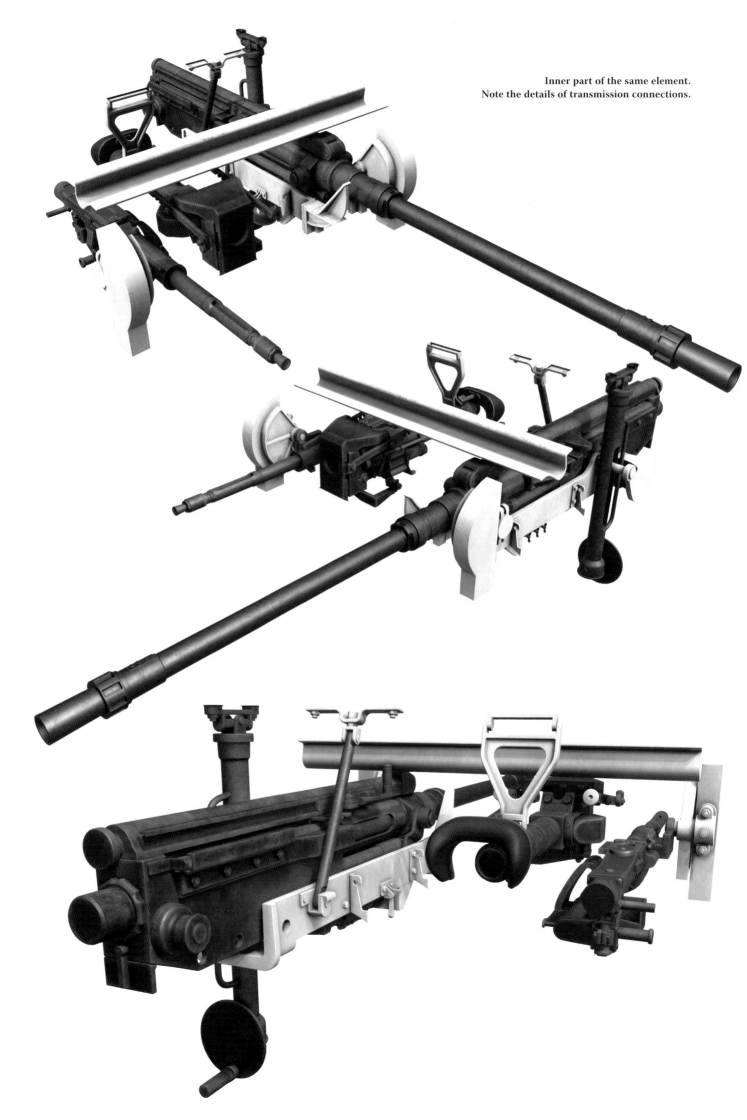

Inner part of the same element.
Note the details of transmission connections.

Pz.Kfpw. II Ausf. F of the German 15. Panzer Division during the North African campaign. The sand yellow paint was applied after the vehicle arrival over the original, dark gray background. The R06 code number suggests probably the command section of one of the armored battalions of that unit.

The major modification of *Pz.Kpfw. II Ausf. F* version was the superstructure front plate. It was changed to the straight one. The turret mount cover was added too.

Left vision port of the driver's compartment as well as a spade mounted on the fender.

Rear view of *Pz.Kpfw. II Ausf. F* with extra stowage boxes clearly visible.

Pz.Kpfw. II Ausf. F was the last variant of the typical Panzer II tanks family. Its construction based inter alia on signals received from the frontline crews. It allowed to make optimum modifications.

Another views of the *15. Panzer Division Pz.Kpfw. II Ausf.* F light tank. It represents the model without another extra stowage box called *Rommel's chest* added on the turret rear plate.

Despite the fact, that since 1942 *Pz.Kpfw. II* tanks had been ineffective in the main frontline combat until the end of World War II they were successfully used for example for reconnaissance.

Right corner view of the *Pz.Kpfw. II Ausf. F* superstructure with the straight front armor plate and a spare road wheel clearly visible.

The rear part of *Pz.Kpfw. II Ausf. F* generally remained unchanged except of some extra stowage boxes added.

Pz.Kpfw. II Ausf. F of the German *15. Panzer Division* rear and front view.

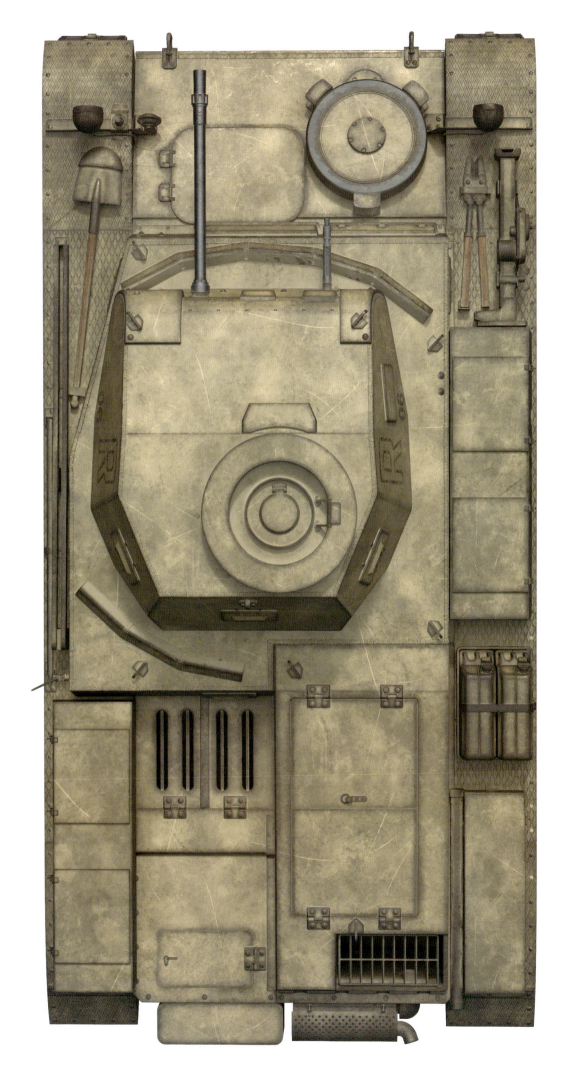

Upper view of the *Pz.Kpfw. II Ausf. F* light tank. Note the extra stowage boxes mounted on the fenders and commander's cupola with eight periscopes.

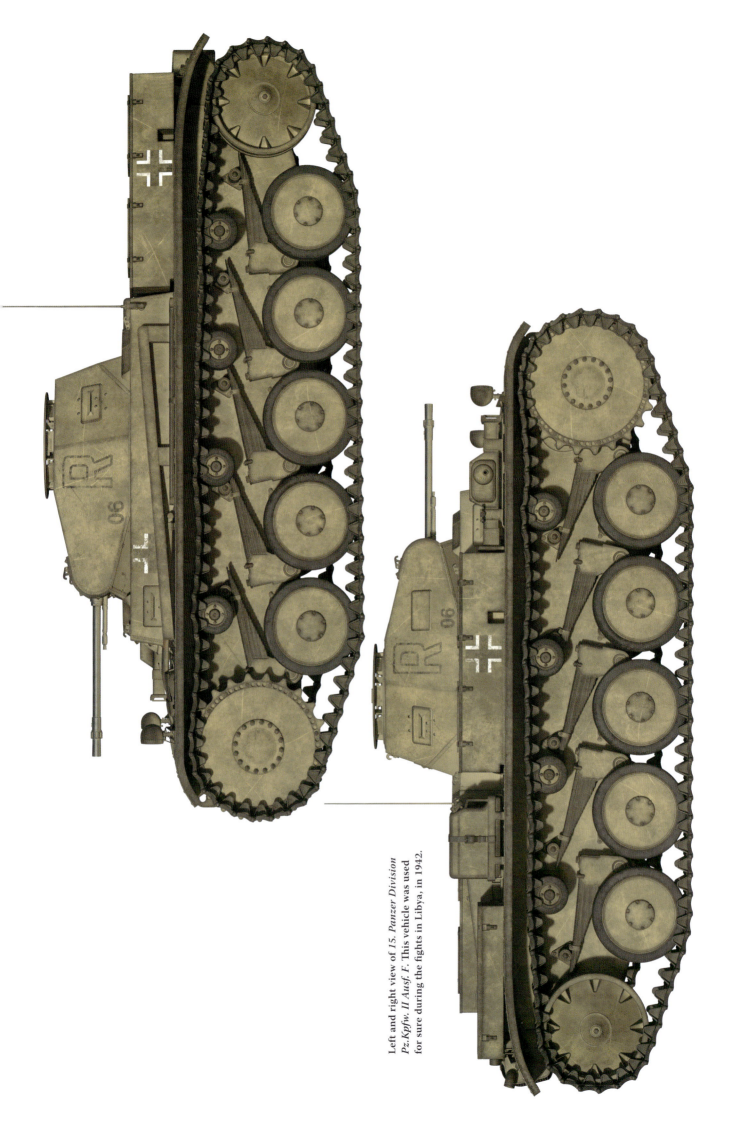

Left and right view of 15. Panzer Division Pz.Kpfw. II Ausf. F. This vehicle was used for sure during the fights in Libya, in 1942.

The light reconnaissance tank *Pz.Kpfw. II Ausf. L Luchs* (*Lynx*) was produced between September 1943 and January 1944 by the MAN factory. The approximately 100 exemplars were completed. The main armament of this vehicle was *2,0 cm Kampfwagenkanone 38 L/55* gun. This particular variant belongs to the German 4th Armored Division during the fights on the eastern front in autumn 1944 and represented the three-tone camouflage scheme implemented more than a year earlier.

Another views of the same tank. It is worth to mention that the *Pz.Kpfw. II Ausf. L Luchs* development began few months before the outbreak of the World War II. The first trial vehicle had been completed in spring 1942 but the production was delayed. This vehicle was similar to the major *Pz.Kpfw. II* family line in name only.

One of the specific features of the *Pz.Kpfw. II Ausf. L Luchs* was the *Schachtellaufwerk* suspension without return rollers.

Pz.Kpfw. II Ausf. L Luchs rear plate with muffler and towing hook. Note the cast towing holes on the edges and *Notek* light.

Upper left view of the *Pz.Kpfw. II Ausf. L Luchs* reconnaissance tank. Compared to the earlier variants of the *Pz.Kpfw. II* vehicles there was a little more space in combat compartment and turret in this model.

Upper right view of the same tank. Note the additional *Sternantenne* installed on the superstructure side and characteristic *Schachtellaufwerk* suspension.

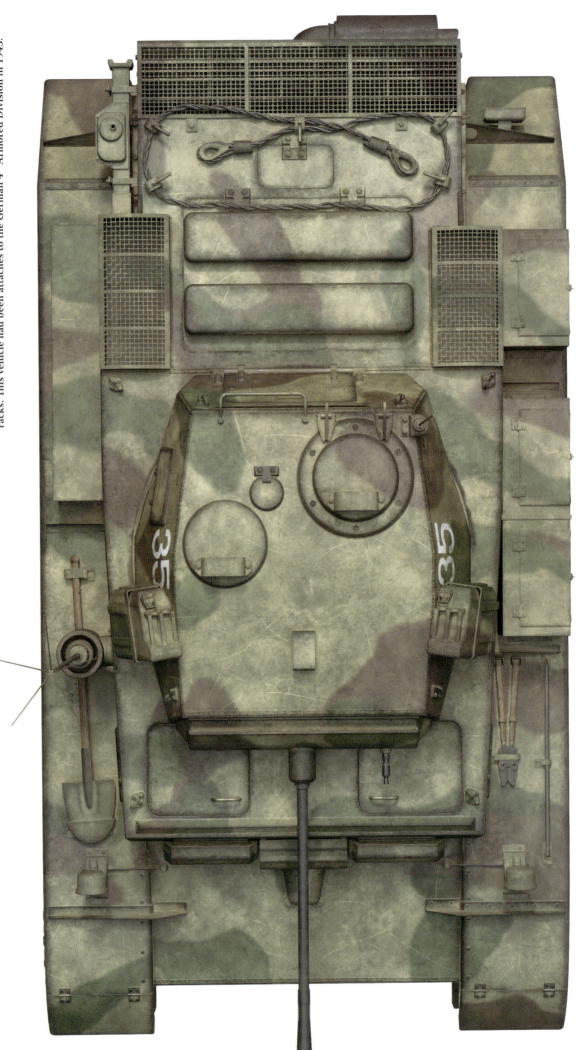

Upper view of *Pz.Kpfw. II Ausf. L*. Note the two turret hatches with periscopes and jerry cans transported in the side racks. This vehicle had been attaches to the German 4th Armored Division in 1943.

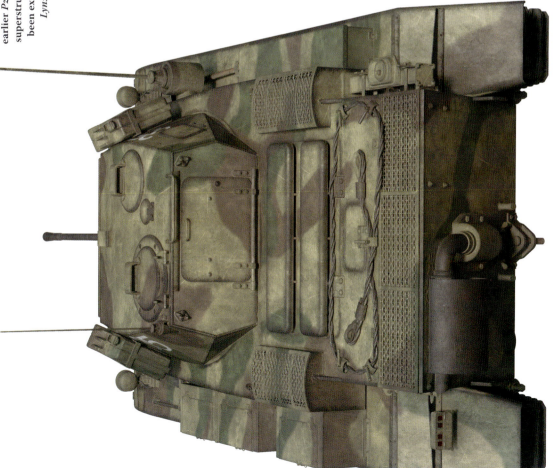

Rear and front view of the same tank. Compared to the earlier *Pz.Kpfw. II* variants the superstructure and turret had been extended. The crew of *Lynx* consisted of 4.

Details of the *Pz.Kpfw. II Ausf. L Luchs* engine deck. The air intakes and towing line are clearly visible as well as jack and a part of muffler.

Details of the *Pz.Kpfw. II Ausf. L* reconnaissance tank turret. This element had been designed strictly for that model and was bigger than the ones installed in the earlier *Pz.Kpfw. II* light tanks. There was also idea to change the 20 mm main gun to the 50 mm anti-tank one but that never occurred.

Details of the *Pz.Kpfw. II Ausf. L Luchs* front part. Some tanks of this variant were also equipped with an extra armor elements strengthening mostly the upper edge of the front armor plate.

The *Pz.Kpfw. II Ausf. L Luchs* superstructure was completely different than the ones installed in case of the other *Pz.Kpfw. II* variants. The driver's and radio-operator's hatches and visors as well as the front light are visible.

Left side of *Pz.Kpfw. II Ausf. L Luchs* turret with jerry can rack and antenna mounting clearly visible.

Buy now
Photosniper
Panzer IV – vol. I, vol. II

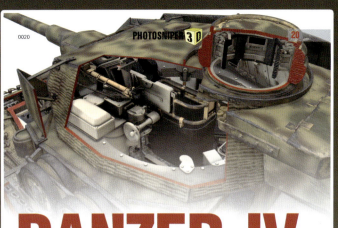
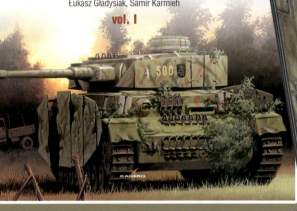

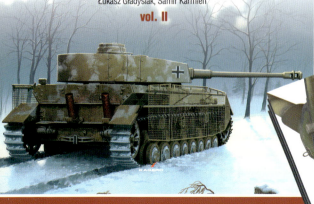

shop.kagero.pl • shop.kagero.pl • shop.ka